YORK NOT[

General Editors: Professo[
of Stirling) & Professor S[
University of Beirut)

Oliver Goldsmith

THE VICAR OF WAKEFIELD

Notes by Brian Donnelly

BA M PHIL (ESSEX)
Lecturer in English, Carysfort College, Dublin

LONGMAN
YORK PRESS

YORK PRESS
Immeuble Esseily, Place Riad Solh, Beirut.

LONGMAN GROUP LIMITED
London
Associated companies, branches and representatives
throughout the world

First published 1980
ISBN 0 582 78114 0
Printed in Hong Kong by
Sing Cheong Printing Co Ltd

Contents

Part 1: Introduction   *page* 5

  The life of Oliver Goldsmith   5

  Composition and publication   8

  The Vicar of Wakefield and its readers   9

  The critical problems   9

  A note on the text   10

Part 2: Summaries   11

  A general summary   11

  Detailed summaries   12

Part 3: Commentary   47

  Contemporary fiction   47

  Purpose in writing *The Vicar of Wakefield*   49

  Social and historical elements in the story   50

  Structure   51

  Plot   52

  The characters   56

  Style   61

Part 4: Hints for study   65

  Points for detailed study   65

  Arrangement of material   66

  Questions and answers: some examples   66

Part 5: Suggestions for further reading   72

The author of these notes   73

Part 1

Introduction

The life of Oliver Goldsmith

Oliver Goldsmith was born at Pallas, County Longford, in the centre of rural Ireland. The exact date of his birth is uncertain, but it was sometime between 1728 and 1731. His father, the Reverend Charles Goldsmith, was a clergyman of the Church of Ireland. He was poor and at one period he had to supplement his income as a curate by farming fifty acres of rented land in order to support his wife and children. Details such as these and the fact that Charles Goldsmith was a kind, generous and unwordly man suggest that he was the model for Dr Primrose in *The Vicar of Wakefield* (1766). He was also the model for the clergyman in Goldsmith's most famous poem, *The Deserted Village* (1770). The village preacher in this poem bears a striking resemblance to Dr Primrose, the Vicar of Wakefield, as can be seen in the following lines:

> *A man he was, to all the country dear,*
> *And passing rich with forty pounds a year;*
> *Remote from towns he ran his godly race,*
> *Nore'er had changed, nor wished to change his place;*
> *Unpracticed he to fawn, or seek for power,*
> *By doctrines fashioned to the varying hour;*
> *Far other aims his heart had learned to prize,*
> *More skilled to raise the wretched than to rise.*

Like the preacher in the poem, Oliver Goldsmith spent his childhood 'remote from towns' and his memories of those years in the Irish countryside became a central element in many of his works. After leaving Ireland as a young man he was destined to spend the rest of his life in cities and the difficulties he endured, especially in London, made him remember his native Irish village as a lost Eden.

In 1745 Goldsmith passed the entrance examination to Trinity College, Dublin. His father did not have enough money to pay for his education so he was accepted as a 'sizar'. This meant that he would receive his food, lodgings and tuition free in return for the performance of such menial tasks as serving meals to the teaching staff and keeping a part of the college grounds tidy. His years as an undergraduate under

these conditions were less enjoyable and beneficial than they would
have been under normal circumstances. No doubt this led to an increased
sense of inferiority which was probably already strong in him owing to
his ugly physical appearance. His face had been scarred by smallpox,
and the portrait of him painted by Sir Joshua Reynolds (c.1770) shows
a protruding upper lip, a receding chin and a dome-like forehead.
Goldsmith's hatred of and contempt for the arrogance and insolence of
the rich and powerful (apparent in his portrayal of Squire Thornhill in
The Vicar of Wakefield) probably began during his years as a poor
scholar in Dublin. As a 'sizar' he was an easy victim for an overbearing
tutor or student to mock and bully.

In 1747 his father died and an uncle helped him to complete his
studies. In 1749 he was awarded the B.A. degree. He spent the following
three years at home, working occasionally as a tutor, and soon showed
that he had inherited at least one of his father's characteristics; he was
completely incapable of managing money. Whatever he earned he spent
with abandon. This generosity and inability to take money seriously
remained with him throughout his life, sometimes with almost disas-
terous results. With his uncle's help he left Ireland in 1752 in order to
study medicine in Scotland, at the University of Edinburgh. This was
to be the beginning of a lifelong exile from his home. Although he never
returned to his native land his memories of it coloured much of his
later work as essayist, novelist, dramatist and poet. During 1752 and
1753 he attended medical lectures at Edinburgh before continuing his
studies at the University of Leyden in 1754. After one year in the
Netherlands he began a walking tour which took him to France,
Switzerland, Italy and Germany. He set out with 'a guinea in his pocket,
one shirt to his back, and a flute in his hand'. His experiences as a
wanderer in Europe was later used in the account of George Primrose's
adventures in Chapter 20 of *The Vicar of Wakefield*. He also drew
upon these experiences in parts of his long poem, *The Traveller* (1765).

Goldsmith arrived in England in February 1756. He possessed a
degree in arts, had some knowledge of medicine and went to London
in search of employment. His jobs were to include working for a chemist,
proof-reading in a printing works and teaching in a school in south
London. During his stay at Dr Milner's school he met the bookseller
Griffin who owned *The Monthly Review*. Griffin offered him a job on
the paper which he accepted. His salary was small but he received free
board and lodgings. This arrangement lasted only six months. Goldsmith
disliked the work, disagreed with his employer, and eventually returned
to his former post at Dr Milner's school. But his short employment
with Griffin was to prove the beginning of his future career as an editor

and man of letters. His early struggles and difficulties as a writer in London were also incorporated into the story of George Primrose's adventures in his novel.

His literary career was in many ways typical of the careers of hundreds of now forgotten writers in the London of the day. By the middle of the eighteenth century there existed an unprecedented demand for the written word. This was caused by a number of factors. These included a growth in literacy among a fairly large section of the population, an increase in wealth making the purchase of books and magazines possible for more people, and developments in the mechanical means of printing to cater for a larger readership. To meet this demand many young men in search of literary fame were employed at low salaries to write essays, reviews and general articles. Few of these 'hacks' ever managed to earn a decent living. George Primrose's account of the period he spent as an aspiring author in London is a vivid and accurate picture of the fate that awaited most ambitious young writers:

> I could not suppress my lurking passion for applause [literary fame]; but usually consumed that time in efforts after excellence which takes up but little room, when it should have been more advantageously employed in the diffusive productions of fruitful mediocrity. My little piece would come forth in the mist of periodical publication, unnoticed and unknown. The public were more importantly employed than to observe the easy simplicity of my style, or the harmony of my periods. Sheet after sheet was thrown off to oblivion. My essays were buried among the essays upon liberty, eastern tales and cures for the bite of a mad dog; while Philantos, Philalethes, Philelutheros, and Philanthropos all wrote better, because they wrote faster than I.

Part of Goldsmith's career was, like that of George Primrose, devoted to the production of essays for magazines and works like *An History of the Earth and Animated Nature*, in eight volumes (1774), which might well have been lost to posterity. That this didn't happen is due to the great success and lasting popularity of *The Vicar of Wakefield, The Deserted Village* and his play, *She Stoops to Conquer*. But this success would never have been achieved had not the greatest man of letters of the period, Dr Samuel Johnson, recognised the spark of genius in this awkward, improvident Irishman. Goldsmith was introduced to Johnson in May 1761 and so began his entrance into the fashionable literary society of the time. He was made a member of the famous Literary Club founded by Johnson and Reynolds in 1763, and Johnson, impressed by his talents, claimed that Goldsmith was 'one of the first men we now have as an author'.

In spite of the recognition of his peers, Goldsmith's career as a writer was never secure or comfortable. His easy ways, generosity and prodigality with money led him into a succession of minor disasters. In fact it was one of his financial crises that led to the publication of *The Vicar of Wakefield.*

Composition and publication

In his biography of Samuel Johnson, published in 1791, James Boswell relates that in the latter part of 1762 Goldsmith was arrested for failure to pay his rent and made an urgent appeal to Johnson for help. Johnson sent him a guinea by messenger and arrived shortly afterwards himself to see what could be done to aid his friend. He asked Goldsmith if he had any writings that could be sold to raise money and Goldsmith produced the manuscript of a 'novel'. According to Boswell, Johnson took the work to Newbery the publisher and sold it for £60 and returned with the money to Goldsmith. However, there is conflicting evidence regarding the sale which suggests that Newbery advanced only twenty guineas for a part share in the book and that other publishers were involved in the purchase. Furthermore, it is by no means certain that the story was completed in late 1762. It is possible that Newbery advanced the money having seen only an incomplete draft of the work. Some scholars believe that it is unlikely that Goldsmith actually completed the work before late 1764. If this was really the case then the long-held belief in a four-year delay in publication is unfounded. One fact is certain: *The Vicar of Wakefield* was published in 1766 in two volumes by a London publisher.

The mystery surrounding the composition and publication of *The Vicar of Wakefield* is very much in keeping with the character of its author and with the work itself. Goldsmith's life and personality were enigmatic. He achieved a literary reputation with unusual speed by eighteenth-century standards and was acknowledged by many to be a writer of rare distinction, even genius. He was befriended by some of the greatest creative personalities of the day and, with the first performance of his comedy, *She Stoops to Conquer*, in 1773, his name became widely known. Yet, in spite of all his successes, he was never fully at his ease during his years in London. He never lost his Irish brogue and seems to have suffered from a sense of insecurity which led him to act the fool in company as a means of disguising his lack of social assurance. In fact he once wrote that 'the true use of speech is not so much to express our wants as to conceal them'. As an Irishman living in London there may even have been an element of contempt in his attitude towards the social and literary circles in which he moved. It is even possible that his notorious buffoonery in company was as much a form of attack against the social norms as a defence against them. He was undoubtedly kind and good-natured, but his ever ready generosity and carelessness about money made the normal management of affairs difficult and sometimes impossible for him. He worked hard and produced an enormous amount of work of very uneven quality beside his famous poems, plays and prose works. When he fell ill in 1774 he insisted upon taking a patent medicine against the advice of his doctors. This childish wilfulness was completely in character. He died on 4 April 1774 after a week of painful sickness.

The Vicar of Wakefield and its readers

Since Goldsmith's death The Vicar of Wakefield has continued to be his most widely read and best loved work. It has also proved by far the most popular of all eighteenth-century novels with readers in the two hundred years since its publication. This popularity is really disproportionate to its achievement as a novel. One reason for this is the absence in it of anything that might prove morally objectionable. It could be given to young readers by adults who felt that contemporary novels such as Defoe's Moll Flanders (1722) or Fielding's Tom Jones (1749) might have a corrupting effect. This was particularly the case in the nineteenth century and in the early part of the twentieth century when moral standards, particularly in sexual matters, were much less flexible than they are today. Another reason for its enduring appeal is its portrayal of idyllic domestic life in a rural setting. As Britain became more urbanised in the nineteenth century many people must have read The Vicar of Wakefield with nostalgia for its attractive picture of a lost rural world where life was less crowded and hurried than it had become in the large cities of a growing industrial nation. The character of the Vicar, Dr Primrose, added greatly to the book's appeal. Indeed there have been few more popular characters in the whole of English literature. It was not only in Britain that The Vicar of Wakefield enjoyed a very wide readership. It has been translated into every European language as well as some non-European ones and, at one period, was used as a text-book in French lycées.

The critical problems

On the surface The Vicar of Wakefield seems to merit this popular and uncritical admiration. Yet it is a book which, when read with attention, reveals some apparent flaws and puzzling complexities. For convenience we call it a 'novel' in that it is a dramatic, prose narrative which appears to present a realistic picture of the life of a group of people in rural England in the earlier part of the eighteenth century. Like most men at the time Goldsmith was a Christian and accepted the Christian philosophy of life as it is revealed in the Bible. His intention in writing the novel was, in part at least, to affirm the virtues of charity, patience, humility and the submission of the personal will to the will of God. This he does, but only by means of an absurd plot which culminates in one of the most contrived happy endings in the whole of literature. There is, too, a very striking discrepancy between the novel's form as a straightforward moral tale and the way in which it is narrated. The story is told by the Vicar and it sometimes seems as if Goldsmith used his narrative ironically in that we occasionally become aware of an important difference between what the Vicar actually says and the way in which the reader is likely to interpret his words. The problem then becomes one of interpretation. Do we accept the Vicar's account of events at face value or are we meant to see this seemingly worthy and noble Christian clergyman as being much less perfect than his own narrative might lead us to believe?

Such difficulties as these never troubled the thousands of ordinary folk who read *The Vicar of Wakefield* for its charming portrayal of rural life or for the moral lessons that it teaches. Yet, even, in Goldsmith's own day there were a few such as Dr Johnson who expressed reservations about the novel. Goldsmith himself was aware of flaws in the novel. In his 'Advertisement' at the beginning of the book he confessed that 'there are an hundred faults in this thing, and an hundred things might be said to prove them beauties'. There is a lot of truth in that remark and it is the task of the student of *The Vicar of Wakefield* to assess for himself precisely where the 'faults' as well as the 'beauties' of the book lie. The major function of this study is to aid the reader in achieving this end.

A note on the text

The Vicar of Wakefield. A Tale was first published in two volumes in 1766. Among the many subsequent editions are those of George Saintsbury, 1866 and O. Doughty, 1928. The novel is included in Arthur Friedman's five volume edition of *The Complete Works of Oliver Goldsmith* Oxford University Press, Oxford, 1966.

Part 2

Summaries
of THE VICAR OF WAKEFIELD

A general summary

Dr Primrose, the Vicar of Wakefield, lives in quiet contentment with his wife and six children. Their life is upset when the Vicar loses his fortune and is forced to accept a post as curate on the estate of Squire Ned Thornhill, a young nobleman with a bad reputation.

Their new life is poor but happy. The Vicar and his son, Moses, work on the small farm to supplement the family income. They are often visited by Mr Burchell, an eccentric gentleman whom they met on the journey to their new home. Their landlord, Squire Thornhill, takes a great interest in the Primrose family, especially in the Vicar's two daughters, Olivia and Sophia.

One evening the family are visited by two fashionable ladies who express an interest in employing Olivia and Sophia as maids. This arrangement falls through, and when it is discovered that Mr Burchell has been instrumental in bringing this about his friendship with the Primrose family comes to an unpleasant end. Towards the end of the story we discover that the mysterious Mr Burchell is really Sir William Thornhill, uncle of Squire Thornhill, and that his behaviour at this point was calculated to protect Olivia and Sophia from his wicked nephew.

The rapid decline in the fortunes of the Primrose family begins when Olivia runs off with an unknown man. The Vicar then begins a long search for his lost daughter and encounters many misfortunes and surprises on his journey. He meets his older son, George, and Miss Arabella Wilmot, George's former fiancée, at the home of a Mr Adams. Squire Thornhill arrives at the house and immediately becomes interested in Arabella Wilmot to whom he soon afterwards becomes engaged to be married. He also buys George Primrose a commission in the army. This apparent act of kindness is really a ploy to keep George away from Miss Wilmot.

On his journey home the Vicar discovers Olivia destitute at an inn and learns that it was Squire Thornhill who seduced her away from home with a promise of marriage. She tells her father that the wedding ceremony that they underwent was a false one intended to mislead her. When the Vicar arrives home with the good news of his daughter's discovery he finds his house on fire. The family escape from the burning building but lose all their possessions. Shortly after this disaster Squire Thornhill insists upon the Vicar repaying his debts to him. As he is unable to do this the Squire has him put into prison and the Primrose family are left almost helpless and destitute.

When he is in prison the Vicar encourages his wife and children to be brave and to put their trust in God. He sets about reforming the other prisoners with great success and makes friends with Ephraim Jenkinson, the scoundrel who had earlier cheated both himself and Moses at the fair. We learn later that Jenkinson had assisted Squire Thornhill in many of his unlawful projects.

To add to the Vicar's suffering Olivia's death is announced and Sophia is abducted by a gentleman while out for a walk. All appears to be lost when George is brought into the prison in chains on a capital charge for having challenged Squire Thornhill to a duel. The Vicar becomes very ill but with the arrival of Sir William Thornhill all is made well again. With the help of Ephraim Jenkinson Squire Thornhill's evil deeds are made known to his uncle, Sir William, who punishes his nephew by confiscating his wealth and possessions. Jenkinson also reveals that the marriage contracted between the Squire and Olivia was really valid and that Olivia, who appears at this moment, was only pretending to be dead in the hope that her father would ask the Squire's forgiveness and so secure his release from prison.

Fortune now smiles on the Vicar and his family. George is forgiven his crime and arranges to marry Arabella Wilmot who had arrived just in time to learn of Squire Thornhill's evil ways and mercenary intentions towards herself. Sir William becomes engaged to marry Sophia whom he had always admired and the Vicar learns that his lost fortune is to be restored to him. The story ends with the weddings of the young couples, Squire Thornhill's attempts to become a better man, and the Vicar reinstated by his fireside with his happy family around him.

Detailed summaries

Chapter One: The Description of the Family of Wakefield; in which a kindred likeness prevails, as well of Minds as of Persons

Dr Charles Primrose, the Vicar of Wakefield, gives an account of himself, his family and their circumstances. He is happy with the simple life of a country priest and takes great delight in his family which includes his wife and their six children. His wife is a kind, good-natured woman and they live a quiet life with occasional visits from their relations. As good Christians they are always willing to give food and rest to the poor without any expectations of repayment. The Vicar says that giving assistance to those in need is one of his greatest pleasures. He says 'so I was by nature an admirer of happy human faces'.

NOTES AND GLOSSARY

This opening chapter provides the reader with the essential background information about the main character in the story. We are given a brief sketch of the Vicar, his family and their place in rural society. However, we learn most about Dr Primrose, who himself tells the story. As a result we see everything through his eyes and are likely to accept his views and opinions as being always right and valid. But to read the book in this way would be a mistake. Goldsmith probably wanted the reader to see that the Vicar is not as innocent and unworldly as he would have us believe. To achieve this Goldsmith used irony. Irony is the use of language in such a way that there is a discrepancy between what is said and the way in which the statement is interpreted by the reader or listener. There is irony in the Vicar's account of the sly way he gets rid of bad relations or troublesome guests and in his reasons for giving George and Sophia their names. In each of these cases Dr Primrose unwittingly lets the reader know that he is not altogether unworldly. Nevertheless, the overall impression which we get of the Vicar in this chapter is of a simple, honest country priest who does his duty and is content with what God has given him.

vicar:	a priest of the Church of England
taken orders:	ordained as a priest
notable:	hard working
contriver:	manager
fortieth remove:	distantly related
pathetic:	emotionally moving
offspring of temperance:	children of a lawful marriage
for handsome is . . :	real beauty is in living a good life
Oxford bred:	educated at the University of Oxford

Chapter Two: Family Misfortunes. The Loss of Fortune only serves to increase the Pride of the Worthy

---

Mrs Primrose is responsible for all household affairs and Dr Primrose devotes himself to his work as a parish priest without taking any payment for duties such as weddings and baptisms. He is preoccupied with marriage and spends much of his time encouraging single men to take wives and married men to remain faithful to their wives. He believes that priests of the Church of England should not remarry in the event of their wives' deaths, a view which is not widely held among other priests. His eldest son, George, is engaged to be married to Arabella Wilmot, the daughter of a wealthy neighbouring clergyman. But this engagement is suddenly broken when it is announced that Dr Primrose has lost all his money because of his merchant's bankruptcy.

NOTES AND GLOSSARY
We are given a further account of the Vicar's domestic life and priestly duties. We learn of his eccentric concern with matrimony and of his son's impending marriage to the daughter of a fellow clergyman. When he learns that he has lost all his money Dr Primrose's principles will not allow him to conceal the fact from Mr Wilmot even though this news will end his son's wedding plans. In this affair we see Dr Primrose's consistency of character. He is honest and charitable and does not allow adverse circumstances to alter his sense of right and wrong. The sudden and unexpected announcement that he has lost his fortune initiates the major development of the plot. Subsequent events will prove a test of his strength of character and allegiance to his Christian ideals in difficult circumstances. The reader may find it useful at this point to summarise the life led by Dr Primrose and his family at Wakefield.

temporal:	worldly
temporalities:	church revenues
curate:	assistant clergyman
Whiston:	a clergyman and professor (1667–1752) at the University of Cambridge who held unorthodox views
monogamist:	one who believes in having only one wife
allowed by all:	everyone agreed
a-hunting:	fox hunting
own:	agree
at large:	in detail
dissembling:	making a pretence

Chapter Three: A Migration. The fortunate Circumstances of our Lives are generally found at last to be of our own procuring

---

Dr Primrose's loss of his fortune is confirmed and he resolves to accept a position as an assistant clergyman in another parish for the small salary of fifteen pounds per year. He hopes to supplement this sum by managing a little farm. His son George is sent to town to find employment, and there is great sorrow at this break up of the family. The villagers are sad to see the Vicar and his family leave as they start out on a seventy-mile journey to their new home. This is a very long journey for them as they had never travelled abroad more than ten miles in their lives before. Having gone forty miles on horseback the family put up for the night at an inn and make the acquaintance of Mr Burchell to whom the Vicar lends money to pay his bill. Burchell accompanies them on their way next day and tells them the history of Sir William Thornhill, the uncle of Squire Thornhill, the young man who is to become Dr Primrose's landlord. During their conversation Sophia falls into a stream and is rescued by Mr Burchell. He wins the gratitude of the young lady and her family.

NOTES AND GLOSSARY
The plot begins to unfold. We encounter the eccentric Sir William Thornhill disguised as a Mr Burchell. This disguise will be revealed later on in the story. We learn of the character of Sir William's nephew, Squire Thornhill. He is reputed to be a lady's man and another element in the plot is introduced—Olivia's unhappy affair with the Squire. The beginning of the love affair between Sophia and Burchell is prepared for in the closing episode of the chapter.

The Vicar's strength of character in helping his family over their difficulty is apparent as well as his indulgence of the little vanities of his wife and daughters. The account of the journey and the Vicar's attitude towards the distance gives us some insight into travel in the eighteenth century.

callous to:	indifferent to
cure:	position as a curate (assistant clergyman)
molestation:	injury
penury:	poverty
patrimony:	fortune, wealth
Hooker:	a famous English clergyman (1554–1600). His great work *The Laws of Ecclesiastical Polity* was published in 1593
Bishop Jewel:	Bishop of Salisbury in the 1570s
assiduity:	eagerness, earnestness
allurements:	attractions
beadle:	parish policeman
ceremony:	formal manners
prevailed upon:	persuaded
sensible:	sensitive
touched him to the quick:	hurt his feelings deeply
profusions:	generosity

importunity:	urgency in demand
approbation:	approval
estimable:	worthy
eccentric virtue:	goodness expressed in peculiar ways
sensations:	feelings
protesting:	arguing
strain:	manner, way

Chapter Four: A Proof that even the humblest Fortune may grant Happiness, which depends, not on Circumstances, but Constitution

---

The Vicar gives an account of his new parish and home. The parishoners are farmers living a simple, traditional life. The family home is plain but pleasant to live in and we are given an account of the day-to-day routine of the Primrose family on their little farm. Dr Primrose and his son work together from sunrise to sunset while the women do the housework. In the evenings they often enjoy the company of neighbours, some of whom sing or play musical instruments. Each day begins and ends with prayer.

We are given an account of the first Sunday morning. The Vicar persuades the women to dress in less fashionable clothes than formerly in order to be in keeping with their new and less affluent position in life.

NOTES AND GLOSSARY
This account of village life reminds one of Goldsmith's description of rural life in his poem *The Deserted Village*. Life in rural England at the time is portrayed as simple and unsophisticated. The people are shown as being in close contact with the important things in life. We see this in their observance of traditional and Christian feast days, in their plain life style and in their good manners. The episode in which the Vicar persuades his womenfolk to wear plainer clothes to church has two functions. It shows the family's difficulty in adjusting to a less comfortable style of life. It also implies that the things which accompany wealth, such as fine clothes, are really unimportant. It is what people really are and not what they appear to be that matters. This is, of course, essential to the moral of the whole work in which so many people disguise their real selves behind a false or pleasing exterior. It may be useful to find other examples of characters who are not what they appear to be in the first three chapters.

opulence:	richness
primeval:	ancient
frugal:	sparing

scarce knew that temperance was a virtue: not aware that they were behaving virtuously by being temperate; unconsciously virtuous

wrought: worked

Christmas carol: hymns sung in the Christmas season to commemorate the birth of Christ (around December 25)

Valentine: St Valentine's day, February 14. The day on which lovers traditionally express their affection for each other

Shrovetide: day before the Christian season of Lent begins. On this day pancakes (a kind of bread) are traditionally eaten

first of April: known as 'April fool's day' because people traditionally play jokes on others to make them appear to be foolish

Michaelmas Eve: the evening before the feast of St Michael, September 29

pipe and tabor: small flute and drum

wit: intelligence

prattling: noisy

good-will: the trade that goes with a business

coppers: cooking vessels made of copper

agreeably relieved: pleasantly satisfied

mechanical forms of good breeding: innate courtesies

we are all bent in gratitude . . .: thanksgiving to God

harmless: simple

lessons: passages from the Bible

poor's box: a collection box for poor people

sumptuary edicts: rules regulating household expenditure

finery: fashionable clothes (the following are all aspects or parts of female clothing: laces, ribands, bugles, catgut, paduasoy, trains, rufflings, pinkings, pathcings, flouncing, sheeding)

mortify: disgrace

pomatum: perfumed ointment

patched: decorated

discretion: good judgement

exigence: state of affairs

trim: dress

hoot: mocking cry

show: ridiculous looking person

frippery: showy dress

plainer cut:	simple style
want:	lack
indigent:	needy
remonstrance:	rebuke

Chapter Five: A new and great Acquaintance introduced. What we place most Hopes upon, generally proves most fatal

---

While enjoying the pleasure of the evening air the Primrose family make the acquaintance of their landlord, Squire Thornhill. The Squire leaves the hunt because he is attracted by the beauty of Olivia and Sophia and spends the evening in their company, singing and playing the guitar. In spite of the efforts of Dr Primrose, Olivia makes her interest in Thornhill plain and is encouraged by her mother who sees the prospect of a successful marriage. Sophia, however, dislikes his imposing manners. When Thornhill has left, Dr Primrose warns them against being too familiar with their landlord whom he distrusts. But neither Olivia nor her mother is convinced by his arguments. Thornhill sends them a side of venison and informs them that he will dine with them in a few days time.

NOTES AND GLOSSARY
This chapter prepares us for the story of the affair between Olivia and Squire Thornhill. We see Thornhill as a presumptuous and arrogant man who is clearly determined to get his own way with Dr Primrose's pretty daughters. The women find his good looks and high social status attractive but Dr Primrose, with characteristic good sense, suspects that behind his pleasing exterior he is really a worthless fellow. However, he is content to warn his womenfolk of the danger without insisting that his opinion is the right one.

The theme of the divergence between appearance and reality becomes central in this chapter. (See commentary on Chapter 4.)

diffused:	spread
centaury:	plant with a red flower
vacant hilarity:	carefree enjoyment
genteel:	well bred
Dryden:	John Dryden, famous poet and playwright (1631–1700)
an age:	a lifetime
fond mother:	foolish mother
fondly:	childishly
hit:	success

Miss Wrinkles:	acquaintances of the Primrose family
damp:	spoil by criticism
familiar:	assuming familiarity
contraries:	opposites
apprehensions:	fears
venison:	meat of deer

Chapter Six: The Happiness of a Country Fireside

As the Primrose family sit down to supper they are joined by Mr Burchell. Mr Burchell enjoyed a reputation as an eccentric who appeared once each year in the neighbourhood and lived with various families. He was always popular with children as he gave them gifts and told stories. After his departure the Vicar expresses regret that Mr Burchell wasted his youth in low company but Sophia and her brother, Moses, defend him, saying that his past reputation is of less importance than his present reformed way of life. The episode ends with Dr Primrose purposely upsetting a pot of cosmetic preparation which the ladies were preparing for the visit of Squire Thornhill.

NOTES AND GLOSSARY
This chapter initiates another thread in the plot when Sophia expresses a more than casual interest in Mr Burchell. The similarities between the mysterious Burchell and Sir William Thornhill are very obvious—both get on well with children and both are willing to do manual work on the farm.

As in previous chapters there is a lot of moralising. That is to say, general moral conclusions are drawn from the behaviour of characters and the fate which befalls them. It is usually Dr Primrose who displays this tendency but in this chapter Sophia and Moses correct the error of his judgement in language identical to his own. The concluding episode in which Dr Primrose upsets the 'wash' pot shows that he is not completely without wordly guile.

warmth:	enthusiasm
universally:	generally
alacrity:	speed and eagerness
confute:	defeat
halfpenny whistle:	small whistle costing one half penny
Buck of Beverland:	an old tale (also, Patient Grissel, The Adventures of Catskin, Fair Rosamund's bower)
alehouse:	an inn
The Greatest Stranger:	Christ

assiduity:	eagerness, earnestness
bagnio:	(*Italian*) house with a bad reputation
pander:	keeper of this house
wit:	cleverness (notice previous usages)
ancients:	Latin and Greek authors
Marsyas:	in Greek mythology the peasant Marsyas almost defeated Apollo in a musical contest and, in anger, Apollo skinned him alive
wash:	cosmetic preparation

Chapter Seven: A Town Wit described. The dullest Fellows may learn to be comical for a Night or Two

Squire Thornhill visits the Primrose family for dinner and engages in argument with young Moses concerning church affairs. His arguments silence Moses and impress the female members of the Primrose family. When Thornhill departs the ladies of the family are enthusiastic about him and his obvious interest in Olivia. Dr Primrose, however, dislikes Thornhill and tries to persuade the ladies that behind his pleasant manners and appearance he is really an undesirable fellow who intends no good.

NOTES AND GLOSSARY

We see Thornhill's charm at work on the ladies but suspect that Dr Primrose is right in his estimation of his character. Thornhill's argument with Moses is full of high sounding words and phrases but he is clearly a man of limited intelligence who humiliates the young boy in order to impress the ladies with his apparent knowledge.

Dr Primrose is seen here as a man of good sense and judgement of character. His womenfolk, on the other hand, are easily led astray by appearances. The reader should consider how the theme of appearance, as opposed to reality, is developed in this chapter.

exhausted:	used up
plumage:	dress
feeder:	groom (one who looks after horses)
by the by:	by the way
pinched:	made poor
'strike me ugly':	an oath
ever:	always
lawn:	fine linen
priestcraft:	ways of priests
analogically:	by means of analogy or comparision

dialogically: in the manners of a dialogue
concatenation: linked
wit: intelligence (see previous usages)
expatiate: talk at length
free-thinker: unbeliever in orthodox Christian doctrines
Thwackum and Square: characters in Henry Fielding's famous novel, *Tom Jones* (1749), who loved to argue with each other
Robinson Crusoe and Friday: characters in Daniel Defoe's famous story *Robinson Crusoe* (1719)
Religious Courtship: a pamphlet written by Defoe, author of *Robinson Crusoe*. In it he discussed the desirability of marrying religious husbands or wives.
Such terms as 'reciprocal duplicate ratio', 'secundum quoad', 'quoad minus' are Latin terms used in learned debate. But here they are used inaccurately by Thornhill.

Chapter Eight: An Amour, which promises little good Fortune; yet may be productive of much

---

Dr Primrose is a little annoyed by the frequency of Mr Burchell's visits and his interest in Sophia. On this occasion Mr Burchell and the Primrose family eat a picnic in the fields and discuss the relative merits of contemporary poetry and the poetry of ancient Rome. Having expressed his dissatisfaction with the poetry of his contemporaries Mr Burchell recites 'A Ballad' as an example of a work free from most contemporary faults. The quietness of the afternoon is disturbed by a shot. Mr Thornhill's chaplain appears with a gun, carrying a dead blackbird which he presents to Sophia. He announces the Squire's intention of giving a ball on the lawn before the Primrose house in the evening and requests Sophia's company at it.

NOTES AND GLOSSARY
The relationship between Sophia and Mr Burchell is developed. His reluctance to attend the ball seems strange until we discover, later on, that he wanted to keep his true identity a secret.

The discussion between Sophia and Moses of Gay's and Ovid's rendering of the Acis and Galatea story is part of a contemporary debate as to the relative merits of the 'Ancient' and the 'Modern' writers. Mr Burchell has a considerable knowledge of both and the ballad which he recites, as well as his views on the shortcomings of much contemporary poetry, probably incorporates Goldsmith's own literary views.

'A Ballad' tells the story of two young lovers, Edwin and Angelina. Angelina believes that Edwin has died as a result of her pretended coldness towards him. Whilst wandering lonely through the woods she meets a hermit and tells him of her sorrow. However, all is made well again when the hermit reveals his true identity as her lost beloved, Edwin.

This story is entitled 'A Ballad' because a ballad is a traditional story told in verse form. Ballads were intended to be sung or recited aloud to an audience. The regular rhythm and rhyme scheme was a device to help make the words easy to memorise in the days before printing was invented.

The fantastic love story as well as Edwin's incredible disguise function as ironic comments on the main plot of the novel.

requited:	repaid
jesting:	joking, playful
wit:	intelligence (see previous usages)
airs:	ways, manners
temperate repast:	simple meal
Mr Gay:	John Gay, a famous poet (1685–1732) and composer of *The Beggar's Opera* (1728)
Acis:	a youth famous for his great beauty in Greek mythology. He was killed by Polyphemus, his rival for the sea nymph Galatea
Ovid:	Latin poet (43BC–AD18)
epithet:	an adjective denoting quality
luxuriant images:	very beautiful verbal pictures
hermit:	a holy man who lives alone and away from the world
taper:	candle
forlorn:	unhappy and alone
forbear:	have patience
phantom:	Will o' the Wisp
scant:	very small
cell:	hermit's small home
scrip:	small bag
spring:	outflow of water from the earth
modest mansion:	hermit's cell
revels:	entertainments
trimm'd:	prepared to light
pensive:	sad and thoughtful
legendary lore:	very old folk tales
habitations:	homes

spurn'd:	rejected
trifling:	of no importance
paltry:	unimportant, insignificant
wretch:	most miserable person
fond:	foolish
bashful:	shy
transient:	of short duration
confest:	revealed
rude:	ungrateful
unhallowed:	unholy, sinful
imputed:	supposed
feign'd:	pretended
proffers:	gifts
constant:	faithful
emulate:	equal
fickle:	unreliable (opposite of constant)
importunate:	persistent
triumph'd:	rejoiced
rends:	tears apart
approbation:	disapproval
report:	sound of a gun fired
ball:	dance
grass plot:	lawn

Chapter Nine: Two Ladies of great Distinction introduced. Superior Finery even seems to confer superior Breeding

---

Mr Thornhill and his party arrive for the ball. When extra chairs and ladies have been found the dance commences. Olivia dances well and becomes the centre of attention, especially the attention of Mr Thornhill. But the evening is disturbed by a number of incidences which Dr Primrose believes to be of a morally doubtful nature: Thornhill suggests that the gentlemen should sit on the ladies' laps, the conversation becomes risqué from time to time and, at the close of the dance, the guests suggest that the Primrose girls should accompany them home. Dr Primrose's refusal to agree to the latter proposal causes the evening to end on an unpleasant note.

NOTES AND GLOSSARY

Thornhill's attempt to seduce Olivia gains momentum. Dr Primrose's suspicions about Thornhill's real intentions are intensified. His wife and daughters, however, are blinded by his superficial charms.

In this episode we get a glimpse of a common rural pastime and a striking contrast between the naïve simplicity of country folk like the Primrose women and the worldly-wise people like the Flamborough girls who have been partly brought up in the culture of the town. This contrast between town and country often appears in Goldsmith's works, especially in *The Deserted Village*.

scarce:	just
under gentlemen:	attendants
rosy:	rosy cheeked
flaunting:	showily dressed
chit:	young person
easy:	relaxed
gazers:	onlookers
owned:	admitted
pat:	in time with
coarse:	rude
the living jingo:	a rude expression
a muck of sweat:	covered in perspiration
into the shade:	out of the focus of attention
mortified us sensibly:	offended our feelings
tip-top:	very best
condescension:	self-conscious attention to an inferior
polishing:	acquiring social graces
nice:	exact, precise
warmth:	anger
coup de main:	sudden attack
seconded:	agreed to a proposal
short:	bad tempered

Chapter Ten: The Family endeavour to cope with their Betters. The Miseries of the Poor, when they attempt to appear above their Circumstances

Olivia and Sophia have their fortunes told by an old gypsy who predicts that Olivia will marry a squire and Sophia a lord. From this onwards hopes of a great future begin to affect Mrs Primrose and her daughters in spite of Dr Primrose's warnings. The ladies insist on going to church the following Sunday on the plough horses but arrive too late for the ceremony because of the unwillingness of the horses to carry their riders.

NOTES AND GLOSSARY

Vanity and the prospect of good marriages have made the Primrose women ignore all Dr Primrose's good advice. The description of their journey to church on the horses is amusing and makes fun of their pretentions to gentility. There is a slight hint of criticism of Dr Primrose's constant preaching to the ladies on the need for 'temperance, simplicity and contentment'. We realise that only experience will teach the lessons that Dr Primrose is at pains to extol in little sermons.

Dr Primrose's gentle mocking of his wife and daughters in this episode shows him to have a subtle sense of humour and irony and an ability to see the limitations of his own influence upon his family. The reader should consider in what way Goldsmith makes the episode of the journey of Mrs Primrose and her daughters to the church amusing.

washes:	cosmetic preparations
gauzes:	very fine fabric
catgut:	material made from animal intestines
mean:	poor
musical glasses:	tumblers which give a musical note when struck
tawny Sybil:	dark-skinned fortune teller
cross her hand . . .:	give her money
closeted up:	shut up in a room
Nabob:	a person who acquired a great fortune in India
latent:	in progress
scrubs:	untidy people
blowzed:	red in the face
smock:	a wide fitting upper garment
plow horses:	horses used to pull the plough
trimmed:	groomed
broke to the rein:	used to wearing reins (carrying riders)
pillion:	passenger saddle for a woman
cudgel:	club

Chapter Eleven: The Family still resolve to hold up their Heads

---

The Primrose family and Mr Burchell spend Michaelmas-eve playing traditional games at the Flamborough house. During one of the games Lady Blarney and Miss Skeggs arrive, to the embarrassment of everyone present. Having enquired after the family they engage in social gossip and happen to mention that they are in need of serving maids. Mrs Primrose, with her husband's approval, suggests her two daughters as suitable candidates for these positions, a suggestion which the two ladies agree to consider.

NOTES AND GLOSSARY

This episode advances the action of the plot. Mr Burchell realises that the two ladies are imposters who are attempting to lure Olivia and Sophia into the grasp of Squire Thornhill. His ploy to stop this happening in a later chapter proves successful but is misunderstood by Dr Primrose.

The silly and pretentious conversation between the two ladies reveals the shallowness of their characters and is yet another of Goldsmith's attacks on so called 'high society' in this book. The name 'Blarney', incidentally, derives from an Irish expression meaning one who is never lost for something to say.

What insights into eighteenth-century English social life do you get in this chapter?

happening:	taking place, occurring
suffered:	allowed
lamb's wool:	a drink made of hot ale
blind man's bluff:	a game in which one of the players is blindfolded and must try to catch one of the other players
weaver's shuttle:	a machine for making yarn from wool
beggar:	do an injustice to
vulgar:	low
hither:	to this place
prolocutor:	spokesman
professions:	friendly gestures
fond of:	likes (see earlier usages)
Knights of the Garter:	an order of noblemen
valet de chambre:	servingman
fudge:	nonsense
Hanover Square:	a fashionable area of London
Lady's Magazine:	journal edited by Goldsmith
quarter:	person
proper:	suitable
pink, point, frill:	aspects of dressmaking
form:	proper way of doing things

Chapter Twelve: Fortune seems resolved to humble the family of Wakefield. Mortifications are often more painful than real Calamities

---

Dr Primrose and his wife discuss their daughters' prospects. Mrs Primrose has great hopes of their advancement in the service of Lady Blarney and Miss Skeggs but her husband is less certain of their future. A little later a servant arrives with the news that their daughters have been highly recommended by Squire Thornhill. Mrs Primrose persuades

Dr Primrose to sell the colt in order to buy a good horse and they decide to allow Moses to trade the animal at the fair next day. When Moses returns they learn that he was tricked into buying a gross of spectacles with the money he received for the colt.

NOTES AND GLOSSARY

This chapter is a good example of the book's humour. The cheating of Moses at the fair is typical of many such episodes in eighteenth-century novels where youth and innocence fall prey to sharp practice. It is, moreover, a variation on the book's central theme of the unreliability of mere appearances and the ease with which youth can be led astray by an attractive façade. Only Mr Burchell has a clear vision of what is going on and he falls foul of Mrs Primrose for having reservations about their daughters' good fortune.

acquaintance of taste: fashionable friends
Entre nous: (*French*) between ourselves
higgles: argues
deal: soft wood used to make furniture
scarce: hardly
commendations: praise
circumspection: care
diffidence: lack of enthusiasm
repartee: argument
wit: logic (see previous usage)
sell his hen of a rainy day: proverb meaning having prudence and caution
touch them off: get the better of opponents
gross: one hundred and forty-four
a fig for: a term of dismissal
murrain: plague
trumpery: nonsense
blockhead: fool
imposed upon: fooled
prowling sharper: ever-ready cheat
prey: victim

Chapter Thirteen: Mr Burchell is found to be an Enemy, for he has the confidence to give disagreeable Advice

---

As a result of Moses's failure at the fair Dr Primrose moralises upon the foolishness of the poor in trying to rise above their place in society and Moses tells the story of the giant and the dwarf.

Once again Mr Burchell expresses reservations about Olivia and Sophia's future employment and raises the anger of Mrs Primrose. As a result of this disagreement he leaves their company. On his departure Dr Primrose expresses his annoyance at his wife's discourtesy to their guest but admits that he had all along been unhappy with Mr Burchell's attachment to Sophia and does not regret his departure.

NOTES AND GLOSSARY

As well as advancing the plot this chapter is of particular interest in its revelation of the character of Dr Primrose. So far in the story he has been a fairly straightforward character with clear and uncomplicated views of right and wrong. However, the incident between Mr Burchell and his wife leads him to suppress the prompting of his conscience in favour of what he regards as being the best state of affairs for Sophia's future well-being. He is momentarily willing to neglect his duty to a fellow man because such a course of action will profit his family. Dr Primrose is aware of his shortcomings at this point as we see in his final remarks on 'conscience'. In this episode he becomes a more complex and more interesting character. (Compare the Vicar's behaviour here with his behaviour in Chapter 2 when he learns of his lost fortune.) The reader should consider what relevance the tale of the dwarf and the giant has to the incidents in the story so far.

coping:	dealing
Saracens:	Arabs who opposed the Christian Crusaders in the Middle Ages
plight:	situation
plain:	a flat area of land
Satyr:	a mythological being, half man, half goat
damsel:	lady
like to have:	likely to be
declare off:	give up
ill a grace:	bad humouredly
assurance:	confidence
low-lived:	having led a bad life
finished:	good mannered
attachment:	interest
aught:	anything
economist:	manager
specious:	false

Chapter Fourteen: Fresh Mortifications, or a Demonstration that seeming Calamities may be real Blessings

In order to raise money for his daughters' departure to their new employment Dr Primrose goes to the fair to sell his second horse. While having a drink at the inn Dr Primrose meets a seemingly wise old man who agrees to buy his horse. However, as he cannot find change for his banknote, he gives Dr Primrose a draft payable on presentation to his friend Solomon Flamborough. When Dr Primrose presents the draft to Solomon Flamborough he learns that he has been duped by the very same man who sold the spectacles to his son, Moses. On his arrival home Dr Primrose finds his wife and daughters in very low spirits as the fashionable ladies have broken the contract because they have received bad reports of the two girls.

NOTES AND GLOSSARY

This is a humorous chapter which makes a serious moral point. We are entertained by the ease with which Mr Jenkinson fools Dr Primrose. However, we see that Dr Primrose, for all his learning and wisdom, is not an infallible judge of character.

The mysterious reports which put a stop to the prospects of Olivia and Sophia advance the story's plot. The reader should compare the way in which Mr Jenkinson cheats Moses in Chapter 12 with his fooling of Dr Primrose in this episode.

deliberation:	discussion
chapman:	peddler
spavin:	disease affecting a horse's lower leg
windgall:	swelling of the lower leg of a horse
hack:	a horse for ordinary riding.
St Gregory:	Pope Gregory I (590–604)
green:	vigorous
bulwark:	defender
dross:	worthless things
broached:	attempted to explain
Sanconiathon, etc.:	ancient scholars
draught (or draft):	an order for the payment of money
truant:	boy who stays away from school
eclipsed:	hidden, blotted out

Chapter Fifteen: All Mr Burchell's Villainy at once detected. The folly of being overwise

---

Mr Burchell's letter-case is found by the Primrose boys and in it the family find a copy of a letter written to the ladies at Thornhill castle. The contents of the letter state that it would be unwise to employ the Primrose girls because they are of low character. So the mystery surrounding the withdrawal of their contract appears to be solved.

Mr Burchell then arrives at the Primrose house and is confronted with his action. But he is totally untroubled by the discovery, to the great annoyance of Dr and Mrs Primrose.

NOTES AND GLOSSARY

As well as advancing the plot, this episode allows for the temporary removal of Mr Burchell from the story as he will not be needed for some time. The discovery of the letter-case and the subsequent arrival of Mr Burchell are typical of the many unlikely coincidences that take place in the story.

The malicious way in which Dr Primrose plans to take his revenge on Mr Burchell shows that he is no saint in spite of his strong Christian principles.

The reader should make a note of any other unlikely coincidences which have already occurred in the story. It would be useful to pick out an example of moralising from this chapter.

seconded:	agreed to
solicition:	request
lewd:	of low morals
admonition:	advice
railed:	spoke angrily against
ruminating:	thinking
cutting:	wounding
shooting of:	pains in
jest book:	book of funny stories
wit:	humorous person (see previous usages)
Pope:	Alexander Pope, famous poet (1688–1744)
mechanic:	manual worker
sublime animations:	lofty creations
particular:	case, instance
pitch:	degree of anger
alarmed:	uneasy
allegory:	symbolic story in which abstracted ideas are represented as living beings

Chapter Sixteen: The Family use Art, which is opposed with still greater

Squire Thornhill pays frequent visits to the Primrose household and shows a deep interest in Olivia. The family have their portraits painted and Thornhill poses with the group, sitting at Olivia's feet. Mrs Primrose decides to force Thornhill to confess his intentions towards her daughter by asking his advice as to the suitability of a neighbouring farmer as a husband for Olivia. Thornhill dismisses this proposal but does not commit himself as Mrs Primrose had hoped.

NOTES AND GLOSSARY

In this chapter we have some of the most amusing episodes in the book. The incident of the family portrait is ironic in that it points out the pretentions of the Primrose family. This is emphasised by the fact that the finished work is too large to fit into their house.

Mrs Primrose's attempts to make the Squire confess his intention of marrying Olivia is a fine example of Goldsmith's skill in writing humorous dialogue. This ability is seen at its very best in his famous comic drama, *She Stoops to Conquer* (1773). Indeed, a scene very similar to that between Thornhill and Mrs Primrose takes place in the play when Mrs Hardcastle encourages her son to marry a young lady.

sensations:	feelings
admit of:	allow
abroad:	away from home
play-houses:	theatres
wits:	comic writers (see previous usages)
by rote:	by heart
piquet:	a card game
sharp:	alert
owned:	admitted
peculiar:	individual
native:	natural
limner:	artist
a head:	each
stolen march upon:	advantage won over
attitudes:	manner of posing for a portrait
genteel:	well bred
Venus:	goddess of love in Greek mythology
stomacher:	article of dress worn over the breast
Cupids:	boys of great beauty. Cupid was identified by the Romans with Eros the Greek God of love, and was represented as the son of Venus.

Amazon:	mythological female warrior
green joseph:	green riding overcoat with a cape
spare:	fit in
Alexander the Great:	famous king of Macedonia (356–323BC)
material:	important
becoming:	appropriate
want for parts:	lack good qualities

Chapter Seventeen: Scarcely any Virtue found to resist the Power of long and pleasing temptations

---

The Primrose family use Mr Williams as a bait to encourage Thornhill to propose marriage to Olivia. But, as Thornhill fails to make any proposal, it is agreed that Olivia should marry Mr Williams in four weeks' time.

A few evenings before the wedding day the Primrose family are enjoying an evening together around their fireside when their happiness is broken by the discovery that Olivia has been abducted by two gentlemen in a post-chaise.

NOTES AND GLOSSARY
The affair between Olivia and Thornhill takes a new turn and the plot is further complicated by the disappearance of Olivia.

Goldsmith uses his amusing poem 'An Elegy on the Death of a Mad Dog' as an excuse for a debate on the shortcomings of some contemporary poetry. (See Mr Burchell's remarks on contemporary poetry in Chapter 8.) This digression is interrupted by the news of Olivia's abduction which serves as the occasion for a discussion between Dr Primrose and his son about the proper Christian attitude towards one's enemies and towards children who err against their parents.

It would be useful to summarise the views expressed in this chapter on the proper Christian attitudes towards enemies and ungrateful children.

own:	admit
suffering:	allowing
your day:	wedding day
cider-press:	machine for making cider, a drink made from apples
brewing tubs:	containers used in making beer
Death and the Lady:	a ballad
Elegy:	a poem expressing sorrow. In this elegy Goldsmith is satirising this kind of poetry
race:	life

pique:	disagreement
vulgar:	common
ode:	a poem with an elevated theme
elegists:	writers of elegies
sensible part:	people with common sense
versify:	write a poem about
sublimer:	loftier
Ranelagh:	a fashionable place outside London
nymphs and swains:	young men and women as represented in traditional pastoral poetry
post-chaise:	horse-drawn carriage
strumpet:	woman of low morals
sallies:	bouts

Chapter Eighteen: The Pursuit of a Father to reclaim a Lost Child to Virtue

---

Dr Primrose's search for Olivia leads him to Squire Thornhill's house and thence to a distant place where he has heard that Mr Burchell and Olivia were seen together. His search proves unsuccessful and on his return journey he becomes ill and is forced to borrow money to pay for his three-week stay at an inn. On resuming his journey he falls in with a group of travelling actors. When they reach the next town a well-dressed gentleman invites them to have supper at his home.

NOTES AND GLOSSARY

The mystery surrounding Olivia's whereabouts deepens. Goldsmith uses Dr Primrose's meeting with the players as an opportunity to express his views on the state of the contemporary drama in which he had a great interest. His meeting with the well-dressed gentleman is the beginning of further complications in the plot.

This and subsequent chapters dealing with Dr Primrose's journey in search of Olivia show Goldsmith employing the form of the picaresque tale introduced into English fiction by Henry Fielding (picaresque comes from Spanish stories of rogues, *picaro* being Spanish for a rogue). The picaresque plot is based on the journey of the hero and the adventures he encounters on the road. Fielding's novel, *Tom Jones*, is a famous example of this kind of fiction.

seat:	country home
elopement:	to run away in order to get married
averred:	testified
the wells:	fashionable health resort

stroke: event
issue of my disorder: outcome of my illness
defray: pay for
philanthropic: charitable
pieces: coins
refractory: stubborn
strolling company: travelling actors
exhibit: perform
Dryden [1631–1700], **Otway** [1652–89], **Rowe** [1674–1718], **Congreve** [1670–1729], **Farquhar** [1678–1707]: all famous dramatists
go down: popular
over-charged: exaggerated
nature: life
shrugged: forced
equipage: carriage
masquerade: assumed, fictional
punch: a hot alcoholic drink
parliament-man: member of parliament

Chapter Nineteen: The Description of a Person discontented with the Present Government and apprehensive of the loss of our Liberties

Dr Primrose and the players return to the home of the well-dressed gentleman where he and Dr Primrose discuss political matters at some length. To everyone's surprise a Mr Arnold and his wife unexpectedly arrive and Dr Primrose realises that his host was merely Mr Arnold's butler taking advantage of his master's absence. Miss Arabella Wilmot, the young lady who had once been engaged to George Primrose, arrives in company with the Adams family and Dr Primrose is invited to remain in the house as a guest.

In the evening Miss Wilmot and Dr Primrose attend a performance given by the players and discover that George has become a member of the group.

NOTES AND GLOSSARY
The encounter of Dr Primrose with the butler provides a way of bringing Dr Primrose, his son and Miss Wilmot together. There is a lengthy digression in which Goldsmith airs his political views in the scene between Dr Primrose and the butler. This exchange of political views has nothing to do with the main events in the story and is likely to prove tedious to the present-day reader. The butler, who pretends to be

the master of the house, is only the latest among several imposters in this story.

The reader ought to see whether he can name all the characters in the story so far who assume disguises?

deshabille: informality of dress
Monitor, Auditor, etc.: papers of different political allegiances
Cornwall: a large area, a county in South-West England
pillory: place for public punishment
declamation: widely expressed opinions
Levellers: a religious-political party in the seventeenth century
                     who advocated a form of communism
subordinate orders: lower classes
men of opulence: rich men
so minded: of the opinion
furnished with: provided with
Cartesian: theory formulated by the French philosopher
                     Descartes (1596–1650)
warmth: enthusiasm
Jesuit: a member of an order of Roman Catholic priests
wooden shoes: slang term to describe foreigners
Fair Penitent: a tragedy by Nicholas Rowe (1674–1718), popular
                     in Goldsmith's day

Chapter Twenty: The History of a philosophic Vagabond, pursuing Novelty, but losing Content

George Primrose gives a vivid account of his travels and adventures since his departure from Wakefield. From London he travelled to Europe and suffered many mishaps on his journey. On these travels he met with a wide variety of people and usually encountered the worst side of human nature. His employment included work as a writer, a tutor, and an itinerant musician. On his return to England he found employment with the players and this led to his meeting with his father and former sweetheart.

NOTES AND GLOSSARY
George's story is a digression. It has very little to do with the main events in the book except in so far as he briefly came into contact with Squire Thornhill and his uncle. The various adventures which he recalls are loosely based on Goldsmith's own experience as a young man after he departed from Ireland in 1752. George's account of his attempts to make his career as a writer in London is an informative piece of

eighteenth-century social and literary history. His mood of disillusionment throughout this chapter probably reflects Goldsmith's own feelings of neglect as a young man. The student may find it useful to make a brief summary of George Primrose's history after his departure from Wakefield.

footmen:	servants
desisted from:	refrained from
revolution:	turn
carolled:	sang
mart:	market
sardonic:	derisive
chalked out:	planned
anodyne necklace:	hangman's noose
under turnkey:	assistant jailer
Newgate:	London prison
cutler's wheel:	knife grinder's wheel
jogg-trot men:	literary hacks
Grub Street:	where poor writers lived and worked in London;
paradox:	a seeming self-contradiction
Propertius:	Roman poet (50–15BC)
beggars in rhyme:	bad poets
Philantos, etc.:	Goldsmith satirises writers of the time by giving them Greek names which mean lover of oneself, of truth, of freedom, of mankind
at the bottom:	in reality
underling:	servant
tattering a kip:	slang: raiding a house of ill-fame
epitome:	perfect example
Chickasaw Indians:	tribe in Alabama, U.S.A.
moveables:	belongings
desideratum:	vacancy
venal:	mercenary
intaglio:	gem with a figure carved into it
cognoscente:	experts
Pietro Perugino:	Italian painter (1446–1524)

Chapter Twenty-one: The Short continuance of Friendship amongst the vicious, which is coeval only with mutual satisfaction

Squire Thornhill arrives at the Adams house and shows immediate interest in Miss Wilmot. He buys George a commission in the army in order to get him out of the way, though this act is construed by George and his father as an act of kindness. Before departing for home Dr Primrose promises to repay Squire Thornhill the cost of the commission at a later date.

On his way Dr Primrose meets his daughter, Olivia, at an inn and discovers that Squire Thornhill, and not Mr Burchell, had led her astray. The marriage ceremony which the couple underwent was invalid. Indeed, Squire Thornhill had already been involved in six previous wedding ceremonies.

NOTES AND GLOSSARY

The true character of Squire Thornhill is revealed. He is a liar and a cheat who is willing to sacrifice anyone for his own pleasure. His plan in removing George Primrose is clearly calculated to secure Arabella Wilmot as his next victim.

Once again we see Dr Primrose's gullibility in his total lack of suspicion of Squire Thornhill's motives in assisting George. We also see his Christian charity and fatherly love in his care for his 'prodigal' daughter.

The plight of Olivia can tell the reader a good deal about the position of women in society at the time. And this chapter shows that the rich had various advantages over the poor in the eighteenth century.

ensign:	a second lieutenant
abatement:	reduction
bond:	pledge
Lord Falkland:	a general in the service of King Charles I. He died in battle in 1643
bedews:	covers with dew
bounty:	generosity
going out of the window:	going broke
as lief:	prefer
budge:	move
the cross of her money:	the colour of her money
sassarara:	beating or scolding
popish priest:	Roman Catholic priests who were forbidden to perform marriage ceremonies at the time

---

Chapter Twenty-two: Offences are easily pardoned, where there is Love at bottom

---

Having secured a room for Olivia at an inn Dr Primrose goes home to break the good news to the rest of the family. He arrives at his home about midnight to find the building on fire. He awakens his family and rescues his two youngest children from the flames.

The neighbours do all they can to assist their distress. They make a temporary home in one of the farm buildings and Sophia and Moses fetch Olivia home from the inn. Mrs Primrose upbraids her daughter for her behaviour but her husband insists that such reproaches must stop. Dr Primrose urges the exercise of charity.

NOTES AND GLOSSARY
Here is yet another disaster in the life of the Primrose family which adds a further burden to Dr Primrose's troubles. The difference in the reception which Olivia receives from her father and her mother dramatises the difference between the characters of the two parents. It also provides an opportunity for a homily on the proper Christian way to receive a child who, having erred, returns home destitute (see the biblical story of the 'Prodigal Son' in Saint Luke's Gospel, xv).

The reader should notice how coincidence is used in this episode.

censures:	accusations
unreproaching:	unaccusing
fond:	pleasant (see earlier usages)
waned apace:	darkened gradually
mastiff:	dog
dilated:	beat
conflagration:	fire
transports:	joy, happiness
untutored:	natural
poignant:	painful
censuring:	hostile, accusing
in countenance:	in good humour
undeviating rectitude:	constant goodness

Chapter Twenty-three: None but the Guilty can be long and completely miserable

Since her return home Olivia has been in low spirits and her father does all he can to encourage her to an acceptance of her situation. But all such efforts result in failure. News arrives that Squire Thornhill is engaged to be married to Miss Arabella Wilmot. Dr Primrose sends a letter to Miss Wilmot to warn her of her danger but as she is away on a visit Moses is forced to leave the note to await her return.

NOTES AND GLOSSARY
The Vicar's philosophical resignation to the mishaps of life shows his strength of character. His letter to Miss Wilmot will only result in the

Squire's anger and will help to lead to the further misfortunes that Dr Primrose has to endure.

qualified:	in a position to
solicitations:	approaches
the power of one:	God's power
base resolution:	bad intention
engrossed:	took up
equipage:	carriage
mouldering:	decaying
similitude:	comparison
langour:	depression
over-wrought:	over-worked

Chapter Twenty-four: Fresh Calamities

Squire Thornhill arrives at the Primrose house with an invitation to his wedding with Miss Wilmot. Dr Primrose staunchly refuses to have anything further to do with the man who has seduced his daughter. His spirited denunciation of the Squire leads to the latter's demand for immediate repayment of the Vicar's rent and the debt incurred in buying George's commission into the army. As Dr Primrose, owing to the recent fire, has no money, his cows are confiscated to meet part of the debt and two officers of the law arrive to take him to prison.

NOTES AND GLOSSARY

The Vicar's misfortunes now become central in the story. His refusal to ignore Squire Thornhill's past actions in spite of the family's pleading and the threat of imprisonment and destitution gains the reader's admiration. He is clearly a man who lives according to his principles and is usually willing to practise what he preaches.

The student should consider the relevance of Sophia's 'little melancholy air' to the events in the story.

concert on the trees:	birdsong
corroding:	rotting
shunning:	avoiding
undone:	incapacitated
insolence:	insulting behaviour
utmost stretch:	full extent
train of accidents:	succession of accidents
rigorous:	harsh
dispatch:	speed

Chapter Twenty-five: No situation, however wretched it seems, but has some sort of Comfort attending it

---

On his way to prison Dr Primrose has to urge many of the poorest members of his parish to refrain from attacking his jailers and securing his release. In prison Dr Primrose is offered some small assistance by a fellow prisoner whom he recognises as Ephraim Jenkinson, the man who had cheated both himself and Moses at the fair. Because of Mr Jenkinson's kindness to him the Vicar promises to intercede on his behalf with his prosecutor, Mr Flamborough, and forgives him the crimes committed against himself and his son.

NOTES AND GLOSSARY
The episode in which the Vicar stops the crowd attacking the officers and his magnanimity towards Mr Jenkinson show his adherence to Christian teaching. The Bible teaches obedience to the law and forgiveness of those who offend against oneself. Dr Primrose lives his life strictly according to such teachings as we see in this chapter and throughout the rest of the book. A question the reader should ask, after reading this chapter, is: how does the Vicar recognise Ephraim Jenkinson?

enfeebled: made weak
divest themselves: remove from themselves
imprecations: insults
transported with joy: very happy
flock: parishioners
I pen my fold for immortality: prepare my people for heaven
wanting: in a state of sin
ancient superiority: former importance
knowing man: natural good sense
dotage: old age
coiner: forger
heavenly corrector: God

Chapter Twenty-six: A Reformation in the Gaol; to make laws complete, they should reward as well as punish

---

Having provided accommodation in the town for his wife and daughters Dr Primrose tries to reform the other prisoners in the jail. At first he meets with laughter from the prisoners but eventually wins their respect.

At supper time Mr Jenkinson joins the Primrose family and relates his life story to them and, in turn, the Vicar tells of the unfortunate circumstances that have led them to the town jail. On hearing this account Mr Jenkinson makes a sudden departure saying he will try to help them.

NOTES AND GLOSSARY
Instead of being dejected by his imprisonment Dr Primrose makes the best of things and performs what he sees as being his duty as a Christian minister by trying to reform the other prisoners. Here we see his courage and simple faith at work.

The unexpected departure of Mr Jenkinson on hearing the story of the Primrose family suggests that he will have a part to play in helping them out of their difficulties. The reader may find it useful to write down a short account of Ephraim Jenkinson's career.

answered very conveniently: suited very well
against to-morrow: to provide for the future
in open arms against: hostile to
tremendous enemy: God
incumbent upon: falling upon
what signifies: what does it matter
past the hour of amendment: beyond hope of reform
parts: appearance
blockheads: fools
the knowing: worldly-wise people
sharper: cheat

Chapter Twenty-seven: The same Subject continued

In spite of his wife's objections Dr Primrose proceeds with his plan of reforming the prisoners. At first they mock him or play tricks on him but in the end he does succeed. Dr Primrose organises them to produce goods for sale outside the prison and so the prisoners begin to make profitable use of their time. As a result of his success Dr Primrose criticises the penal code of the country. His chief objections to it are that it punishes without attempting to reform the criminal and, because the sentence of death is often passed for minor offences, it fails to make proper distinctions between serious and minor crimes.

NOTES AND GLOSSARY
The Vicar's optimism is rewarded. His criticism of the penal code shows much good sense. Indeed his belief that the function of imprisonment should be to reform rather than to punish the criminal is a viewpoint

often expressed by liberal minded people at the present time. Here Goldsmith is clearly expressing his own views through the character of the Vicar.

disapprobation:	disapproval
the gulf:	state of sin
sensibility:	proper feelings
tobacco stoppers:	used to press down tobacco in pipes
capitally punishing:	the death penalty
untutored nature:	natural, uncivilised instincts
refined:	civilised
moroseness:	bad temper
gibbets:	gallows for hanging criminals
dross:	base metal
refiner:	one who refines or makes pure
sinew:	strengthen

Chapter Twenty-eight: Happiness and Misery rather the Result of Prudence than of Virtue in this Life; temporal Evils or Felicities being regarded by Heaven as things merely in themselves trifling, and unworthy its care in the distribution

---

Olivia becomes ill and eventually dies, and Dr Primrose's letter to Squire Thornhill requesting clemency is ignored. Sophia is abducted by a gentleman while out walking and Dr Primrose grows ill himself. His one comfort amid all this misfortune is a letter from his eldest son telling of his great progress in the army. But just as the family has finished reading the letter George is brought bleeding into the prison. He is under sentence of death for having challenged Squire Thornhill to a duel on having learnt of Squire Thornhill's conduct towards the family in a letter from his mother. All seems lost as Dr Primrose's letter to Sir William Thornhill asking for his aid has received no reply.

NOTES AND GLOSSARY
The fortunes of the Primrose family are now at their lowest and all seems lost. Dr Primrose's fortitude begins to break and it is only by the encouragement of Moses and George that he is able to look upon things with Christian patience and humility, putting his life in the hands of God. This short lapse into weakness on the part of Dr Primrose makes his character more human and therefore more convincing to the reader.

The student should try to retell, in his own words, the very unlikely coincidence which occurs in this chapter.

longed:	desired

expiring: dying
incumbent on me: my duty
eternal tribunal: God's judgement
an abode that looks brighter: Heaven
postillion: a man riding one of the two or more horses drawing a carriage and controlling that pair or the leaders (OED)
lieutenancy: rank in the army
countermanded: confined to barracks
baggages: slang term of endearment
arrogate: to take upon oneself without right
greatest tribunal: God's judgement (see above)
niggardly: mean

Chapter Twenty-nine: The Equal Dealings of Providence demonstrated with regard to the Happy and the Miserable here below. That, from the nature of Pleasure and Pain, the Wretched must be repaid the balance of their Sufferings in the Life hereafter

---

Dr Primrose delivers a sermon to his family and to his fellow prisoners from his sickbed. He speaks of the hardships of life, the need for religion in order to endure life's trials, the great rewards that the poor and weak will enjoy after death, rewards which the rich and powerful can never experience to the same degree. He asks them to look upon death as a release into a better existence. Those who enjoy the good things of this life may fear death, but the wretched of the earth have nothing to lose and a lot to gain.

NOTES AND GLOSSARY
In this sermon Dr Primrose expresses an attitude towards this world that lies at the very heart of Christian thought and teaching. It is an attitude that is often found in the Bible (see, for example, Revelation 21: 4–6: 'And God shall wipe away all tears from their eyes; and there shall be no more death, neither sorrow, nor crying, neither shall there be any more pain: for the former things are passed away . . .'). His manner of delivering this sermon is in the traditional style of English Christian pulpit oratory.

The student should summarise Dr Primrose's criticism of philosophy.

wretched: poor and weak people
heavy-laden: those who must suffer hardship and sorrow
the poor man in the parable: refers to the Bible, Saint Luke's Gospel 16:25

Chapter Thirty: Happier Prospects begin to appear. Let us be inflexible, and Fortune will at last change in our Favour.

Sophia arrives at the prison in the company of Mr Burchell who has helped her to escape from her captors. Mr Burchell's true identity is made known to the surprise and embarrassment of the company. He listens to the story of the misfortunes that have befallen the Primrose family since he last saw them. He forgives George his rash act and sets about discovering the identity of Sophia's abductors.

NOTES AND GLOSSARY
Events begin to move swiftly and with the appearance of Sir William Thornhill a happy ending to all the family's troubles is in sight.

a transport of affection: overjoyed
canvas:	covering of a coach window
menaces:	threats
shivered:	broke into pieces
the air:	manner
hazards:	risks
apprised:	informed
party:	all political opinions

in the commission of the peace: a magistrate
secure:	guarantee
compliance:	agreement
apothecary:	dispensing chemist

Chapter Thirty-one: Former Benevolence now repaid with unexpected Interest

---

Squire Thornhill arrives at the prison and is justifying his behaviour to his uncle, Sir William, when Mr Jenkinson enters with the Squire's henchmen and exposes him as a scoundrel. Sir William learns of all the evil doings of his nephew. Arabella Wilmot comes upon the scene and also learns of the infamy of her future husband. She agrees to marry her true love, George Primrose, but Squire Thornhill says he will not return her dowry. However, George is content to marry her without any marriage portion. Just at this point Mr Jenkinson ushers in Olivia Thornhill who had really been in hiding in the hope that her father, believing her to be dead, would agree to beg forgiveness from the Squire. Mr Jenkinson surprises Squire Thornhill by producing a certificate of marriage between him and Olivia. He, Mr Jenkinson, admits that he had hired a real priest to perform the marriage ceremony and not a false one as the Squire had thought. He did this in order to be in a position to blackmail Squire Thornhill in the future. Everyone is happy with the outcome except the Squire, who must forfeit Arabella Wilmot's dowry and finds himself married to Olivia. His uncle, however, has mercy on him. He grants him a small allowance and exhorts him to make a new life with Olivia. All ends happily when Sir William takes Sophia as his future wife and Mr Jenkinson, in spite of his former evil ways, is given £500 for his good services to the Vicar and his family.

NOTES AND GLOSSARY

Here we get the happy ending that the previous chapter has led us to expect. All mysteries are solved and everyone is content with the outcome. In this episode Goldsmith displays great ingenuity in the way in which he manages to assemble all the main characters together in one place for the final resolution of the complications of the plot. As a piece of 'stage management' it hints at Goldsmith's skill as a writer for the theatre and reminds one of the technique of modern writers of crime fiction, especially Agatha Christie. The student will find it useful to summarise the main events in this chapter in the order of their occurrence.

wanted:	went without
Baronet:	Knight
equitable:	legal
Tyburn:	place of public execution in London
circumstantial:	detailed
viper:	poisonous snake
fostering in my bosom:	taking care of
prosecution:	legal proceedings
consummated:	performed
decorums:	proper behaviour
indigence:	poverty
the cloth:	the church
the giver of joy:	God

Chapter Thirty-two: The conclusion

Sir William Thornhill, Sophia, George Primrose and Arabella Wilmot are married by Dr Primrose in the church after some slight confusion as to which couple should be married first. The happy couples and their relations then enjoy the marriage feast at the inn. Earlier that morning Dr Primrose learnt that his merchant had been discovered in Antwerp and that a considerable portion of his lost fortune would be restored.

We learn that Squire Thornhill is living with relations and is well on the way to becoming reformed. Olivia confesses to her father that she may even be willing to forgive the Squire.

The story ends with everyone in high spirits and the Vicar expressing his gratitude that fortune has treated him so well.

NOTES AND GLOSSARY

All trouble and dissension is at an end and the unity and harmony among people is symbolised in the double marriage. This ending is in keeping with the oldest conventions of 'comedy' in English literature. Other notable examples are to be found in the comedies of Shakespeare.

There is a moment of gentle humour when Dr Primrose attempts to create an air and mood of solemnity on the way to the church without any success.

The student should examine the number of meanings given to the word 'wit' throughout the story.

effects: possessions
deportment: personal behaviour
refractory: unmoved
protesting: exclaiming
half a guinea a piece: ten shillings and sixpence each
digress: move away from the main point in a story or conversation
wit: intelligence (see earlier usages)

Part 3

Commentary

Contemporary fiction

From the time of its publication *The Vicar of Wakefield* has been referred to as a 'novel'. The use of the term 'novel' in this case simply implies that the book is an extended narrative which tells the story of a number of characters and the adventures that they undergo. It also suggests that these characters and the world which they inhabit are, more or less, like people and places which the reader might have encountered in real life.

The term 'novel', however, was beginning to acquire a more precise meaning by the middle of the eighteenth century when Goldsmith wrote *The Vicar of Wakefield*. It gradually came to suggest a work of fiction which faithfully imitated the real world in which men live. This helped to distinguish it from earlier works of fiction which can be referred to as 'romances'. The large number of 'romances' written in Europe since the Middle Ages also told of the adventures of characters. But they differed from the kinds of fictions which we today think of as novels in one major respect. The laws which governed the lives of the characters in these early fictions did not always imitate those of the real world in which their authors lived. Giants and witches, for instance, often inhabited the world of the romance along with human characters. The supernatural usually governed the actions of the characters and an ending in which the heroine was snatched from the hands of an evil being by some form of divine intervention was typical of many of these stories.

The eighteenth-century novel gets its name because, to a large extent, it broke away from the conventions of the romance. Indeed the very term 'novel' implies something which was new, Goldsmith's friend, Dr Johnson, saw that significant changes were taking place in the prose narratives of the day. In an essay in 1750 he described the new kind of writing as follows:

> The works of fiction with which the present generation seems more particularly delighted, are such as exhibit life in its true state, diversified only by accidents that daily happen in the world, and influenced by passions and qualities which are really to be found in conversing with mankind. (*The Rambler*, no.4)

Johnson here pointed to the chief characteristics of the novel which may be summed up as follows:

(*i*) It gave a true picture of real life in its setting and characterisation.

(*ii*) The laws governing human behaviour are such as might be experienced in the lives of ordinary men and women (therefore, such things as supernatural beings and direct mystical interference in men's lives are largely excluded from the novel's terms of reference.)

(*iii*) The touchstone of the novelist's art is the real world of experience.

It is true that not all eighteenth-century novelists adhered strictly to the demands of 'realism'. Indeed most novels of the period contain episodes which seem to the reader unlikely if not downright impossible. But when we read such works as Daniel Defoe's *Robinson Crusoe* or Henry Fielding's *Tom Jones* we see that for the first time in English prose fiction the writer has attempted to portray character within the framework of man's real social experience. Such characters as Crusoe or Tom Jones interest us because they are ordinary people who encounter the ups and downs of life and are shaped and developed by their experiences. Like real people their characters are not static but respond and grow to the demands made of them by life. In comparison with these men the characters in most earlier works of fiction are unrealistic in the literal sense of the term. They rarely grow and develop but tend to remain exactly the same at the end as they were at the beginning of their adventures.

Most writers of earlier romances were more interested in the outside agencies that govern man's life than they were in the characters who people their stories. In the Middle Ages this reflected current philosphy. Man was seen as a being who fitted into a divine plan for the world and was therefore uninteresting when set against the supernatural forces that shaped his destiny. By the beginning of the eighteenth century an important change had already taken place in men's thinking. The absolute certainties of the medieval world view had disappeared. Throughout the whole of Europe a new spirit of individualism could be detected, a spirit which was discernible in the seventeenth century and which found expression in the philosophy of Locke and Descartes. One of the major effects of this new thinking was the belief that the individual could discover truth for himself through his senses. Unlike men in the Middle Ages, eighteenth-century men no longer believed in a divine plan which could be rigidly applied to all men in every situation. The interest in character as reflected in the novels of writers like Richardson, Defoe and Fielding was, to a large extent, a result of the change in men's thinking about themselves and their role and destiny in the world.

When he came to write *The Vicar of Wakefield* Goldsmith was familiar with the relatively new forms of fiction which were becoming popular at the time. But he was even more familiar with all the traditional and popular forms of narration. There was

(*i*) The 'romance' with all its old formulas of sudden disasters, unexpected and inexplicable events and the return of good fortune at the end.

(*ii*) There was the 'picaresque tale' in which the hero sets out on a journey and meets with many adventures along the way before his safe return home.

(*iii*) There was also the narrative used as a framework for philosophical or theological debate between characters such as Johnson's eastern tale, *Rasselas* (1759).

Novelists such as Defoe, Fielding and Smollett employed elements of these traditional forms and adapted them to their own purposes. So, too, did Goldsmith in *The Vicar of Wakefield*. His book shows the influence of each of the forms of narrative listed above, yet the way in which he adapted them to his purpose raises a number of important critical problems not found in the work of those novelists who also employed and modified the older fictional forms. (These are discussed in the section on character and plot.)

Purpose in writing *The Vicar of Wakefield*

It is difficult to say exactly what purpose Goldsmith had in mind when he wrote *The Vicar of Wakefield*. In fact it is unlikely that he had any one single reason for composing the work other than the obvious one of making enough money to live on for a few months. Certainly it gave him the opportunity to put aspects of his own personal experience into fictional form. At the outset it would appear that his main intention was to compose a moral and didactic tale which would impress upon the reader the great Christian virtues of patience, charity, humility and obedience as these are exemplified in the character of Dr Primrose. This at any rate is how it has been interpreted by generations of readers in Britain and Europe since it was published. But, we must ask ourselves, is it as simple as that? Was Goldsmith, perhaps, gently mocking or making fun of his idealised portrait of the Vicar? Is *The Vicar of Wakefield* to some extent a satire upon the kind of didactic tale that it so innocently appears to be on the surface? *The Vicar of Wakefield* is a fascinating and puzzling book because it forces us to ask these questions. The later sections on the plot and the characters deals with them at some length.

Social and historical elements in the story

The Vicar of Wakefield does not claim to give an accurate or detailed picture of England or English rural life in the first half of the eighteenth century. Nevertheless, it does to some extent reflect the social realities of the period.

As has already been mentioned, Goldsmith based much of the story on his own personal experiences. It is fairly certain that the character of the Vicar, the Reverend Charles Primrose, is modelled upon his own father, the Reverend Charles Goldsmith, who was a clergyman in the Church of Ireland. Much of the author's own experiences are used in the story of George Primrose's travels on the continent of Europe and his period in London. The discussions about poetry in Chapter 8 and the information about the contemporary theatre in Chapter 18 reflect Goldsmith's own career as a poet and dramatist. The arguments about monarchy in Chapter 19 are taken from his history of England published in 1764.

No one is certain about the real location of the village of Wakefield or of the Thornhill estate. It is probable that Goldsmith had no specific places in mind when he wrote the story but drew a picture of a typical English village community of the period. The village of Auburn in *The Deserted Village* is not a specific place but a generalised description that incorporates the typical features of most English villages at the time. The same is true of his description of life in *The Vicar of Wakefield*. Like the Auburn of the poem it is a generalised picture of a village and is probably coloured by Goldsmith's memories of his own native village in Ireland.

Goldsmith's portrayal of the hierarchical structure of his rural community is historically fairly accurate. The local Squire owned most of the lands on which the community lived. He was therefore the most powerful man in the area and, although he had not got the power of life and death over the people, he still, as a rule, had the forces of the law biased in his own favour. Goldsmith was always keenly aware of the abuses which this system lent itself to as we can see in *The Vicar of Wakefield* and in *The Deserted Village*. Our memories of the corrupt Squire Thornhill are likely to be more vivid after reading the book than what we remember of his good uncle, Sir William.

The episodes involving the Primroses reflect the family structures of the time. The father was the absolute head and women were considered to be inferior to men. But, as we see in the story, women were allowed a good deal of freedom and often obtained their own ways by subtle means. The domestic bliss which the family enjoy in the early chapters of the novel is very much an idealised portrait of family life in a rural setting. It is perhaps the most attractive part of the whole novel and has added greatly to its lasting popularity.

In the eighteenth century the Church of England was a central social as well as spiritual force in the land and Dr Primrose is always fully aware of his role in society. As a minister he occupies one of the central positions in the community. However, his unswerving dedication to the laws of his religion is hardly typical of most clergymen at the time. Like the rest of men they were a mixture of good and bad and, in eighteenth-century fiction, we meet as many scoundrels as saints in the role of clergymen.

Finally, it is worth emphasising that Christianity was part of the whole fabric and way of life for eighteenth-century men and women. They may have obeyed or ignored the teachings and laws of Christ as revealed in the Bible. Few, however, seriously doubted the Christian view of the world. Dr Primrose exemplifies that view in its purest form. In his eyes God controls everything that happens to man. Even when the greatest disasters befall him he is prepared to submit to them as being the will of his creator. Therefore, patience and humility are seen as great virtues. Along with these man must be charitable. This demands that he show mercy to all men, even to his worst enemies as Dr Primrose does consistently in the story.

Structure

By the term 'structure' we mean the general design of a work of art, the way in which its parts are related to one another in the formation of the whole work.

The Vicar of Wakefield is a very carefully planned book. Its proportions are almost symmetrical in design:

(*i*) There are thirty-two chapters.

(*ii*) The first three chapters serve as an introduction to characters and events.

(*iii*) The final three conclude events and contain the denouement.

(*iv*) This leaves twenty-six chapters in between and they are evenly divided. Thirteen precede Olivia's flight (the turning point in the story) and thirteen follow up to the final climactic chapters.

This well-proportioned structure was hardly accidental and seems to refute the notion that the story was composed in a careless or whimsical fashion. If we accept that Goldsmith gave some care to the planning of his work then it has serious implications for the way we interpret his apparently careless plot and, ultimately, his real intentions in writing the book.

The two parts of the narrative are very different. The first is light-hearted. In spite of the Vicar's loss of his investment and forced departure from Wakefield life remains pleasant and serene. There is a good deal of comedy and we are given loving sketches and vignettes of idyllic family life in the country. In the second half the Primrose family undergo a series of disturbing experiences. Catastrophe follows hard upon catastrophe. The quiet mood of the earlier part of the story disappears and is not re-established until the final chapter when, once again, the Vicar sits patriarch-like amidst his family before a cosy fire.

Plot

If we judge it by the standards of a realistic novel the plot of *The Vicar of Wakefield* is absurd and inept. Dr Johnson accurately suggested that the new kind of fiction (Fielding's novels) portrayed 'life in its true state, diversified only by accidents that daily happen in the world ...'. (see section on contemporary fiction). In other words, all the events that take place should be plausible by the kinds of laws that govern man in his normal daily life. By that standard *The Vicar of Wakefield* is a total failure, as a brief analysis of some of the unlikely happenings will show.

(*i*) The hasty departure of the Vicar and his family from Wakefield is not adequately explained.

(*ii*) The role played by Sir William Thornhill defies belief on the part of the reader. He is said to be only thirty years of age which makes him, implausibly, almost the same age as his nephew, Squire Thornhill. He is a rich man but when the Vicar first meets him pretending to be Mr Burchell he cannot pay his bill at the inn. He spends most of the novel on his own lands under his assumed name, yet, oddly, none of his tenants recognise him. Most strange of all there is no good reason why he does not put a stop to his nephew's designs upon the Vicar's daughters. In the final prison scene, he incredibly appears to be ignorant of the full extent of Squire Thornhill's evil ways and requires proof before he punishes the wayward nephew.

(*iii*) The story abounds in the most incredible sequence of coincidences and contrived situations. For instance, many moments of happiness or peace are no sooner established than they are suddenly disrupted by fate. The news of Olivia's abduction in Chapter 17 is revealed just as the Vicar calls upon his wife to fetch another bottle of wine to celebrate their good health and happiness. Dick's announcement of the bad news follows immediately upon the following speech by Dr Primrose: 'Yes, Deborah, my dear we are now growing old, but the evening of our life is likely to be happy'. Much the same thing occurs in Chapter 28. No sooner has Dr Primrose read the letter from George telling of his success in the army than George is thrown into prison beside his father, all bloody and bound in chains, facing a capital charge.

A lengthy list of unlikely coincidences could be made (see summary of the plot pp.11–12.) These unusually involve the sudden arrival of characters in the most unlikely places at improbable times. The final three chapters in which all the main characters are gathered together in the prison is typical of a pattern that runs throughout the book.

Goldsmith must have been fully aware of these 'flaws' in his story. To argue that he wrote carelessly or was incapable of managing a realistic plot seems very unlikely. His narrative is too precisely constructed (see section on 'Structure' pp.512) and the stage managing of the final episodes in the prison is too skilful to allow such arguments to carry any weight. It seems probable that, rather than being a failure, the contrivances in the plot were intentional. But, if this was indeed the case, what implications has it for the way we interpret the book's meaning?

There are two possible answers to the problem. They can be summed up as follows:

(1) Goldsmith wrote the story with tongue in cheek. He was in fact being ironic in his portrayal of Dr Primrose and the work as a whole is a kind of parody of romantic fiction.

(2) Goldsmith had no one single intention in writing the book. A good deal of it is mocking or ironic in its treatment of character and the conventions of fiction which it employs. However, it is fundamentally a portrait of a good and kind, if somewhat silly old clergyman. Furthermore, its emphasis on the Christian virtues of charity, patience and submission of the personal will to the will of God is wholly serious.

A full discussion of each of these points of view must wait until the next section as they depend very largely upon our interpretation of Dr Primrose's character. With regard to the plot, however, it appears certain that we are intended to see the contrived nature and mechanical formulas of many of the highly improbable incidences that occur. The way in which Olivia's abduction is announced, for instance, is so unlikely that it draws attention to its very improbability. As in other episodes, such as George's arrival in prison, the disaster is contrived to follow immediately upon the only really happy moment that the family enjoy during the Vicar's imprisonment. In fact a pattern is established so that when something good occurs we know that some disaster is about to follow as when, in Chapter 22, the Vicar rushes home to tell of his discovery of Olivia only to see his home go up in flames.

In episodes like that Goldsmith seems to be making fun of romantic novels by parodying the plot formulas used in that kind of fiction. External evidence also supports this view. He had a poor opinion of the novel as a genre and, on one occasion, advised his brother in a letter not to allow his son to read romances or novels as they depicted a happiness which has never existed. In an essay in *The Bell* he expressed a lack of enthusiasm for Fielding's *Tom Jones* and *Joseph Andrews*, two of the really original and innovative works of eighteenth-century fiction.

Even if we confine ourselves to the text of Goldsmith's novel we discover ample evidence that the author intended a good deal of parody. This is also evident in the language spoken by the characters in many of the scenes of sudden reversals or revealed identity and motive. Goldsmith often underlines the purely artificial nature of the plot by putting equally artifical words into the mouths of his characters. For example, when Arabella Wilmot learns of the real character of Squire Thornhill in Chapter 31 she exclaims: 'O goodness . . . how have I been deceived! . . . Good heavens! . . . how very near have I been to the brink of ruin! But how great is my pleasure to have escaped it!' This, like the mechanics of the plot in the episode, is a splendid parody of the stilted, unreal language of the heroine in much contemporary romantic fiction. (For a fuller discussion of this aspect of the work see the section on 'Style', pp.61–4).

If we allow that the plot of *The Vicar of Wakefield* is self-consciously mechanical then there is a lot to admire in Goldsmith's handling of its machinery. The jail scenes in the closing chapters are brilliantly contrived. The author manages to get all his main characters together in one place with ease and maximum dramatic effect. This skill was to find a more appropriate outlet some years later in his two plays, *The Good Natur'd Man* (1768) and *She Stoops to Conquer* (1773).

In *The Vicar of Wakefield* Goldsmith also used the traditional narrative devices of the picaresque and the philosophic tale (see section on 'Contemporary fiction', pp.47–9). The picaresque tale, which came into English fiction via Spanish, Italian and French literature, structures the plot loosely around the wanderings of the central character. Most of the best known English novelists of Goldsmith's day made use of this convention. The travels of the Vicar (Chapters 18–22) in search of Olivia, and George Primrose's account of his years as a 'philosophic vagabond' in Chapter 20 are in the picaresque manner.

In the philosophic tale (the best example in English is Johnson's *Rasselas* (1759)) the writer is less concerned with character and events than he is with abstract ideas. In this kind of writing the author manipulates his plot in order to get his characters engaged in discussions or reflections upon such topics as art, religion, philosophy, history, etc. Many episodes in *The Vicar of Wakefield* serve as occasions for Dr Primrose to discuss ethics or Christian morality with his family and friends or to give an impromptu homily on a point of Christian doctrine. The book abounds in these episodes but a few examples here will make the point:

(*i*) The Vicar's attitude to Mr Burchell's past life in Chapter 6 occasions an interchange between the Vicar and his children on the merits of reform and the need for forgiveness.

(*ii*) When the Vicar confronts Mr Burchell with his letter in Chapter 15 the encounter between the two men begins with a discussion on integrity and ends with the Vicar delivering a short speech on 'guilt and shame'.

(*iii*) The episode in Chapter 19, in which the butler pretends to be the master of the house, provides an opportunity for a lengthy discourse on politics.

(*iv*) The Vicar's experiences in prison leads to a prolonged outburst on the evils of the penal system in Chapter 27 and to a sermon on the superiority of religion over the consolations offered by philosophy in Chapter 29.

Every reader will be able to point to many similar instances where the action is used as a peg upon which to hang a long, abstract discourse or argument. However, it is often difficult to be sure how seriously we are meant to take these passages of moralising or moral debate. In the case of the Vicar's criticism of the way criminals are punished there is little doubt that Goldsmith is wholly serious, in keeping with the importance of the subject. The penal system and criminal laws of the mid-eighteenth century left much to be desired, and it is noticeable that in this episode the prose has the simple yet eloquent directness of Goldsmith's best essays:

> And it were highly to be wished that legislative power would thus direct the law rather to reformation than severity; that it would appear convinced that the work of eradicating crimes is not be making punishment familiar, but formidable. Instead of our present prisons, which find or make men guilty, which enclose wretches for the commission of one crime, and return them, if returned alive, fitted for the perpetuation of thousands, it were to be wished we had, as in other parts of Europe, places of penitence and solitude, where the accused might be attended by such as could give them repentance if guilty, or new motives to virtue if innocent.
>
> (Chapter 27)

On the other hand, in Chapter 19, the Vicar's long and weighty discourse on monarchy and liberty is made to appear ridiculous when it is revealed that his host is really the butler pretending to be the master of the house. Again, in the episode in Chapter 15 where the Vicar confronts Mr Burchell with the letter, he dismisses the latter in a stagey kind of biblical rhetoric before launching into a short homily on 'Guilt and Shame'. But is not this set speech calculated to underline the Vicar's hypocrisy in his treatment of Mr Burchell? The fact that we are made to think about the surface appearance of characters in this way is an indication of Goldsmith's subtlety in this work.

It is necessary to mention one final point with regard to the plot. A small number of slips occur which suggest that Goldsmith was either careless or wanted to tease and perplex the reader. The most obvious of these slips is that the Vicar refers to his youngest children as 'babes'. Yet, at one point, Mrs Primrose reminds him that he is old and he has told her that they are both old. Another lapse occurs when Dr Primrose refers to 'the Whistonian controversy' and the 'hard measure' that was dealt to him by the archdeacon. Although this seems an important incident it is the first we have heard of it or of the archdeacon.

The characters

Dr Primrose—The Vicar of Wakefield

The book is in a double sense the story of the Vicar. He tells the story and he is the central character in most of the events that he narrates.

When we first read the book he seems to be a very straightforward character.

(*i*) He is a kind and loveable old gentleman who lives a life in accordance with Christian teachings.

(*ii*) He is simple and unwordly. These fine qualities make him an easy prey for men like Mr Jenkinson and Squire Thornhill. His wife and daughters are often able to get their own way in spite of his authority. Yet they love and respect him.

(*iii*) He is often foolish and pompous. Occasionally he is amusing. Nevertheless, he is a man of great physical and moral courage as we see in the prison scenes. These attributes make him admirable in the eyes of the reader. His courage and his endearing charm cause the reader to overlook his little faults and mistakes.

It is these qualities of the Vicar's that have caused the book to be loved and admired by generations of readers. The Vicar radiates true goodness, a very rare quality in literature or in life. His story is, moreover, a parable of the triumph of goodness over evil in the world and as such appeals to most readers. We all like our fictions to acknowledge that there exists in the world a moral order behind the apparent chaos. Our personal experience rarely supports this craving for order. Fiction often does. We all like a happy ending to a story and the tale of the Vicar's rise and fall provides the kind of assurances we desire.

However, is Goldsmith's story as simple and obvious as the above summary of the Vicar's character implies? In the discussion of the plot (pp.52–7) it was suggested that it was not quite so straightforward as it might appear on first reading. In fact there is a good deal of evidence to suggest that Goldsmith was ironic in his portrayal of Dr Primrose. That is to say, he implied that there is often a difference between how the Vicar appears on the surface and his real underlying intentions and motivations. In other words, his character is not quite what it may first appear to be. This should not cause too much surprise when we remember that *The Vicar of Wakefield* is a novel that abounds in disguise or false appearances (see summary of plot). Many of the characters are not what they first appear to be—Mr Burchell, Squire Thornhill, Mr Jenkinson. To what extent is the Vicar himself less saintly than he seems to be?

In the very first chapter Dr Primrose unconsciously reveals that he is not as simple and direct as his account of family life would have us believe. He says that he welcomes any friend or stranger as a guest to his house but tells us that he has a trick for ridding himself permanently of undesirable visitors. His ploy, he informs us, is to lend such a guest 'a riding coat, or a pair of boots, or sometimes a horse of small value, and I always had the satisfaction of finding he never came back to return them. By this the house was cleared of such as we did not like; but never was the family of Wakefield known to turn the traveller or the poor dependant out of doors'. He is a charitable man but his charity is selective and governed by personal likes and dislikes. A little later he informs us that his eldest son, George, was named 'after his uncle, who left us ten thousand pounds'. He then adds 'In less than another year we had a daughter again, and now I was determined that Grissel should be her name; but a rich relation taking a fancy to stand godmother, the girl was, by her directions, called Sophia; so that we had two romantic names in the family; but I solemnly protest I had no hand in it'. In spite of his final disclaimer this admission clearly reveals that the Vicar is much more a man of the world than he would like us to believe. He is too wise to offend rich relations in spite of his preference for the name Grissel over Sophia.

These little shortcomings are hardly major failings but they do suggest a man whose motivations are less than saintly. They do, moreover, prepare us for the Vicar's less than honourable treatment of Mr Burchell. In the initial stages of his acquaintance with Mr Burchell the Vicar finds him to be a pleasant and well-bred man. Yet he is always at pains to discourage his friendship with Sophia. His initial objection is that Mr Burchell has misspent his youth. But it soon becomes apparent that his real coolness towards Mr Burchell springs from economic rather than moral considerations. The Vicar conveniently lays aside his reservations about Squire Thornhill in the expectation of securing him as a son-in-law and, when the opportunity arises in Chapter 15, he severs his friendship with Mr Burchell on the single pretext of the letter. Viewed in this light his speech about 'Guilt and Shame' at the end of the chapter has the air of hypocrisy about it. Earlier he acknowledged his true attitude towards Mr Burchell. After Mr Burchell leaves the house following a disagreement with Mrs Primrose the Vicar comments:

What Sophia's reflections were upon this occasion, I can't pretend to determine; but I was not displeased at the bottom that we were rid of a guest from whom I had much to fear. Our breach of hospitality went to my conscience a little; but I quickly silenced that monitor by two or three specious reasons which served to satisfy and reconcile me to myself. The pain which conscience gives the man who has already done wrong is soon got over. Conscience is a coward, and those faults it has not strength enough to prevent, it seldom has justice enough to punish by accusing.

There is, too, something less than admirable in the way the Vicar allows

Mr Williams to be used as bait in order to encourage Squire Thornhill's interest in Olivia.

Looked at in this way Dr Primrose is certainly no saint. There is, in fact, a good deal of hypocrisy and calculation in his behaviour. Nevertheless, to suggest that Goldsmith intended his portrait of Dr Primrose to be wholly ironic or satiric is just as misguided as the suggestion that he is the embodiment of absolute goodness. The truth lies, surely, in between these two extreme interpretations. The following seems a more balanced and adequate summary of his character:

> The Vicar is a good man even though he can be silly and pretentious. He has a number of human failings and his behaviour from time to time is hypocritical. Yet, by and large, he is a man of real integrity and great courage as we see in his defiance of Squire Thornhill in Chapter 24 and in his fortitude during his prison sentence. His character is more complex than any simple assessment of his role in the novel could suggest and this in itself is a tribute to Goldsmith's artistry in *The Vicar of Wakefield*.

With the exception of Ephraim Jenkinson none of the other characters has any real depth or complexity. They are more or less stereotyped. They never change or develop. This is largely due to the fact that Dr Primrose tells the story and concentrates his analysis of events upon his own reaction to them and upon the intrinsic interest of the events.

Deborah Primrose—the Vicar's wife

The Vicar tells us in Chapter 1 that 'she was a good-natured notable woman' of limited but adequate education. One of the ironies of the Vicar's account is that he is unaware of the extent of the shortcomings that he reveals in his wife's character. She is over-ambitious for her daughters and is willing to sacrifice anything that gets in the way of their marriage prospects. She is unconcerned about Squire Thornhill's reputation. In her estimation he will make a good 'catch' for Olivia. She insults Mr Burchell when he suggests that the proposed employment of Olivia and Sophia may not be in their interests. On such occasions she appears sharp-tongued and shrewish. She is foolish and shallow and often makes herself and the family seem ridiculous as in the scene where they ride the horse to church and in the episode where she tries to make Squire Thornhill confess his interest in Olivia. Such events are among the most humorous in the novel. Indeed, the latter is a fine example of Goldsmith's handling of comic dialogue.

She lacks her husband's spontaneous generosity and charity as we see in her reception of Olivia after her return from Squire Thornhill.

Olivia Primrose

The Vicar's older daughter. She is a beauty and a flirt. Her only desire is to get a husband. She is the kind of 'stock' character often portrayed in contemporary romantic fiction.

Sophia Primrose

The Vicar's younger daughter. She lacks the very striking beauty of Olivia but is less shallow and superficial. Her modesty is rewarded in marriage to Sir William Thornhill. This contrast between Sophia and Olivia is also a 'stock' property of romantic fiction. The same formula is found in the stories in many women's magazines today.

George Primrose

The Vicar's eldest son. He is well educated, brave and handsome and has some of his father's good qualities such as his integrity and sense of honour. His adventures in London and on the Continent makes a pleasant and informative diversion in the story.

Moses Primrose

The Vicar's fourth child and second son. He has received a good, classical education at home. He is a mixture of innocence and maturity. Like his father he enjoys learned discussion but lacks a knowledge of the world. He is easily gulled by Ephraim Jenkinson at the fair. He becomes the breadwinner for the family when his father is in prison.

Ned Thornhill—The Squire

Thornhill, the Vicar's landlord, is nephew and heir to Sir William Thornhill. He is dependent upon the good will of his uncle for his wealth. He is a thoroughly unprincipled young man whose chief interest in life is the pursuit of women and pleasure. He is completely unscrupulous in his dealings with others as we see in his treatment of the Vicar.

However, he is a character without any real depth—a 'stock' figure of evil who is not really frightening to the reader. The last glimpse we get of him suggests that Goldsmith looked upon the character of Ned Thornhill as an absurd, stylised villain. He is portrayed attempting to learn the French-horn as part of his programme of reformation.

Mr Burchell—Sir William Thornhill

Uncle of Ned Thornhill. He is the very antithesis of his nephew. He is a perfect Christian gentleman, well-bred, charitable, friendly and dignified. His disguise is part of his eccentricity. It also enables him to see people in their true light as they make no attempts to impress him in his less elevated role as Mr Burchell. Much of his behaviour is inexplicable, especially his failure to stop his nephew's abduction of Olivia Primrose.

Arabella Wilmot

Daughter of a neighbouring clergyman and a wealthy heiress. She lacks interest as a character but plays a significant part in the workings of the plot. She is engaged to George Primrose at the opening of the story and later becomes engaged to Squire Thornhill who wants to get her fortune. She accepts George Primrose once again and marries him at the end of the story.

Ephraim Jenkinson

A skilled confidence trickster and master of disguises. He gulls both the Vicar and his son, Moses, at the local fair. These are among the most humorous episodes in the whole novel. The trickster who cheats the innocent and naïve is a common figure in much eighteenth-century fiction.

Mr Jenkinson's true identity is made known to the Vicar in prison and he plays an important part in the working out of the plot. In spite of his former evil ways he is a fascinating and entertaining character. The Vicar succeeds in making him abandon his life of crime. However, the reader feels that once he is loose again Mr Jenkinson will employ all his considerable skills upon unsuspecting visitors to fairs.

Style

Style is one of those words in the vocabulary of literary criticism that is often used in vague and imprecise ways. So it is necessary to be as exact as possible and to say what we mean when we talk about the style of any writer or literary work.

In general, style means the way language is used. The term refers to a writer's handling of all the linguistic resources available to him in the composition of his novel, poem, play or essay. In a short work such as an essay it may be possible to point to a predominant style. We may say, for instance, that in his famous letter to Lord Chesterfield (1755) Dr Johnson employs the style of ironic, polite address. By this we would mean that Dr Johnson used the civilised forms of address of an inferior to a superior in such a way that the reader would realise that he was being the very opposite of polite. But in a long work like a novel there will be a wide variety of linguistic usages: direct speech, indirect speech, descriptive passages, the narrator's commentary on the action, etc. Each of these aspects of the work will probably be in a different style. This is the case in *The Vicar of Wakefield*. Because he tells the story, the Vicar's style predominates except in those episodes, such as George's account of his travels in Chapter 20, where he reports exactly what other characters said. The Vicar himself has no one single style but uses language in a variety of ways. These may be categorised as follows: (*i*) a ponderous and pompous use of language which is used more for its sound and effect than for its meaning; and (*ii*) a plain, direct and simple use of language which is both eloquent and to the point.

The Vicar's modulation between these styles is part of the book's meaning. When he is most sympathetic his language tends to be straightforward and dignified, as in his words to Squire Thornhill in Chapter 24:

> 'Mr Thornhill,' replied I, 'hear me once for all: as to your marriage with any but my daughter, that I never will consent to; and though your friendship could raise me to a throne, or your resentment sink me to the grave, yet would I despise both. Thou hast once woefully, irreparably, deceived me. I reposed my heart upon thine honour and have found its baseness. Never more, therefore, expect friendship from me. Go, and possess what fortune has given thee, beauty, riches, health, and pleasure. Go, and leave me to want, infamy, disease, and sorrow. Yet humbled as I am, shall my heart still vindicate its dignity, and though thou hast my forgiveness, thou shalt ever have my contempt.'

His language here is formal and poised, yet it is simple and to the point. There is no seeking after effects. The rhymical flow of the sentences reflect the clarity of the Vicar's thoughts as he argues his position. Here, too, we see a characteristic of his speech as revealed throughout the book; his use of epigram. An epigram is a short sentence which embodies thought or statement in a very compact or pithy way as, 'and though your friendship could raise me to a throne, or your resentment sink me to the grave, yet would I despise both', or, 'and though thou hast my forgiveness, thou shalt ever have my contempt'.

This epigrammatic use of language can be found in most of the Vicar's conversations or discussions. The reader will be able to discover many epigrams for himself. However, two examples taken from Chapter 13 will illustrate the point further:

> Such as are poor and will associate with none but the rich are hated by those they avoid and despised by those they follow.
> Conscience is a coward, and those faults it has not strength enough to prevent, it seldom has justice enough to punish by accusing.

The Vicar's plain, direct use of language is very apparent at the opening of Chapter 23. The words and phrases are often archaic by modern standards but the meaning is clear once we have overcome this difficulty. On occasions, however, his style is highly formal and eloquent as in his sermon to the inmates of the prison in Chapter 29. His words on the hardships of life and the consolations offered by religion are a fine example of Anglican pulpit oratory at its best. The tone is elevated above ordinary speech, the exposition of the argument is contained in lucid, rhythmical periods, and the whole achieves the dignity of memorable speech. Here, too, the Vicar's epigrammatic turn of phrase gives to his utterances the appearance of irrefutable truths:

> My friends, my children, and fellow sufferers, when I reflect on the distribution of good and evil here below, I find that much has been given man to enjoy, yet still more to suffer.
> Death is slight, and any man may sustain it; but torments are dreadful, and these no man can endure.

On the other hand, much of the Vicar's habitual moralising is stale and full of clichés. Often, as in his exhortations to his children to live more humbly at the opening of Chapter 3, his words seem wooden and artificial. Indeed, Goldsmith cleverly parodies this kind of stilted, mechanical speech by making his children moralise in terms indistinguishable from their father in Chapter 6. When the Vicar is insincere, as in his dealings with Mr Burchell, his language reflects this insincerity. In Chapter 15 he says to Mr Burchell: 'Ungrateful wretch, begone, and no longer pollute my dwelling with thy baseness. Begone, and never let me see thee again: go from my doors ...'. Many of Goldsmith's contemporaries would immediately recognise this as the false, melodramatic language of current romantic fiction. If we compare his speech here with his words to Squire Thornhill quoted above the difference is as striking as the difference in the Vicar's moral position in the two episodes.

Goldsmith parodies this kind of melodramatic language to great effect in the closing of the novel. His denouncement is as artificial as any found in melodramatic romance and his parodies emphasise his awareness of this fact. The following sentences are obvious examples:

> 'Heavens', cried Sir William, 'What a viper have I been fostering in my bosom! And so fond of public justic too as he seemed to be. But he shall have it; secure him, Mr Gaoler—yet hold, I fear there is not, legal evidence to detain him.'
> 'Good heavens!' cried Miss Wilmot, 'how very near have I been to the brink of ruin! But how great is my pleasure to have escaped it! Ten thousand falsehoods has this gentleman told me!'

No one ever spoke like that outside the pages of the most banal fiction. By employing the linguistic formulas of such works Goldsmith mocks them and, more significantly, points to the unreality of his own inventions.

As his future writings for the stage were to prove, Goldsmith had an acute ear for comic dialogue. His ability to portray the ridiculous and absurd in human behaviour through the characters' speech is evident in several episodes in *The Vicar of Wakefield*. It is evident in the pleasant banter between the Vicar and his wife in Chapter 10 and we see it again in the conversation between Lady Blarney and Miss Carolina Wilhelmina Amelia Skeggs (the latter's name is in itself a wonderful comic invention) in Chapter 11. Nowhere, however, is Goldsmith's handling of conversation used to such fine comic effect as in the scene in Chapter 16 in which Mrs Primrose tries to force Squire Thornhill to confess his intention of marrying Olivia:

> 'but, sir,' concluded she, 'I should be glad to have your approbation of our choice.'—'How, madam,' replied he, 'my approbation! My approbation of such a choice! Never. What! Sacrifice so much beauty, and sense, and goodness, to a creature insensible of the blessing! Excuse me, I can never approve of such a piece of injustice! And I have my reasons!'—'Indeed, sir,' cried Deborah, 'if you have your reasons, that's another affair; but I should be glad to know those reasons.'—'Excuse me, madam,' returned he, 'they lie too deep for discovery' (laying his hand upon his bosom); 'they remain buried, rivetted here.'

Even such a brief analysis as the above of the variety of styles in *The Vicar of Wakefield* indicates the range of Goldsmith's inventiveness with language. It also suggests that the novel is no straightforward moral tale but a complex and many sided work of art.

Part 4

Hints for study

THE BEST WAY to study *The Vicar of Wakefield* is:

(*i*) Read the novel through without reference to the summaries or to the commentary in these notes. You should, however, use the glossaries after each summary and supplement these with a good dictionary such as *The Concise Oxford Dictionary*. It is also advisable to make your own synopsis of each chapter as you read it. This will help you to retain the story in greater detail.

(*ii*) Having read the book in the above way, re-read it, consulting the summaries in Part 2 on each chapter as you go along.

(*iii*) Study the critical commentary in Part 3. It is advisable to reread the episodes referred to or discussed in detail in this section.

Points for detailed study

For convenience we can divide the major points for close study into the following categories although it should be remembered that there is a good deal of over-lapping in such divisions and a discussion of any one of these may involve reference to one or more of the others:

(*i*) **Characters—Characterisation:** The part played by each of the characters in the story, their chief characteristics (e.g. good, evil, wise, foolish, humorous, etc.) and how they interrelate with the other characters. The way they are portrayed by the author.

(*ii*) **The plot:** How the story is organised in terms of the things that take place and the way in which these events work out in the conclusion. In considering the plot you should be able to discuss the relevance of any single episode to the overall development of the story.

(*iii*) **Narrative:** The way the story is told and the importance of this for our understanding of characters and events. In *The Vicar of Wakefield* any consideration of the narrative will involve an assessment of the Vicar who tells the whole story.

(*iv*) **The portrayal of eighteenth-century rural life:** Consideration of such things as the role of the Squire, the place of women in society, the part played by Christianity in the life of the community, the role of a clergyman, moral attitudes to sex, means of travel, etc. (see Part 3. 'Social and historical elements in the story').

(*v*) **The novel's humour:** Incidents such as the journey to church on the horse in Chapter 10, the visit of the ladies in Chapter 11, the gulling of Moses and the Vicar by Mr Jenkinson in Chapters 12 and 14, the painting of the family portrait and Mrs Primrose's conversation with Squire Thornhill in Chapter 16. You should also consider why these scenes are humorous, what part they play in the story, as well as the use of dialogue in them.

(*vi*) **Major themes:** These are (*i*) innocence v. experience; (*ii*) the triumph of good over evil; (*iii*) appearances v. reality.

Arrangement of material

(*i*) Make your central points at the opening of your essay.

(*ii*) Try to devote a single paragraph to the development of each point.

(*iii*) Illustrate your answers by referring to specific scenes in the novel or, if relevant, by suitable quotations. You may not remember exactly the words used in the text but a concise and accurate paraphrase will do instead.

(*iv*) Try to write as simply as possible and avoid writing long sentences. Keep to the point in your answers and avoid the temptation of discussing aspects of the work which have nothing to do with the question just to show you know about those aspects.

Questions and answers: some examples

The following is intended to give you some idea of the kind of questions you might be asked in an examination and the way you could formulate your answers.

Discuss the character of the Vicar

Dr Primrose, the Vicar of Wakefield, is the main character in Goldsmith's novel. He is also the novel's narrator and we see everything through his eyes except when he reports directly what other characters said. This is a point to keep in mind because his narration governs the view of events that we get in the story.

The Vicar is a kindly old clergyman and a good Christian. He is the father of a large family and his greatest joy is to sit at his fireside with his children around him. He has a tendency to moralise about almost every event that occurs and this occasionally becomes tedious. However, he has a good sense of humour and irony, as we see, for example, in his discussion with Olivia and Sophia about their marriage prospects in Chapter 10.

The Vicar always puts his trust in God and this helps him to endure many hardships such as the loss of his money and position in Chapter 2. But when he falls foul of his new landlord, Squire Thornhill, he loses everything he possesses and is cast into prison for debt. The Vicar had always shown great fortitude in adversity, especially in the case of his daughter's abduction and disgrace, but so many disasters occur in the second half of the story that he almost despairs. His other daughter, Sophia, is abducted, he is told that Olivia has died, and his son George is put into prison on a capital charge. He then becomes very ill as the result of a wound received when rescuing his small children from the fire in their house.

In the end, his faith and trust in God help him to withstand all of these calamities, and his courage is rewarded. With the help of Ephraim Jenkinson and the intervention of Sir William Thornhill, the evil ways of his landlord are made known and his reinstatement to his family fireside in the final chapter is seen as a fitting reward for his courage and trust in the ways of God.

However, the portrait of the Vicar is not completely sympathetic. At times he appears to be more worldly, even cunning, than he would have us believe. His account of how his children's names were chosen in Chapter 1 reveals that he was not uninterested in money. At the end of Chapter 6 he slyly overturns the container of 'wash' that his wife and daughters were preparing for cosmetic use and comments that it seemed accidental and that it was too late to prepare another. His treatment of Mr Burchell in Chapter 15 is largely dictated by his concern for Sophia's marriage prospects. In this episode the Vicar appears to be a hypocrite.

The Vicar is the only complex character in the novel. All the other characters are 'flat'. They never change or develop but remain the same from beginning to end with the possible exception of Ephraim Jenkinson. The Vicar does, to some extent, have something of the depth of a real person as we see in his attitudes to Mr Burchell in Chapter 13. But even he remains largely the same from start to finish. The harsh experiences of the world hardly alter him. No doubt this is one of the reasons why generations of readers have found the book attractive. The Vicar embodies a sense of permanent values in a changing and uncertain world.

The plot of *The Vicar of Wakefield* defies belief. Discuss.

If we judge events in *The Vicar of Wakefield* by the laws of probability that govern real life then, indeed, the plot of the novel often appears to be ridiculous.

There are five stories in the plot. The main one is the story of the family fortunes and it is in reference to this that the other four take place. These are the affair between George Primrose and Arabella Wilmot, the affair between Olivia and Squire Thornhill, the affair between Sophia and Mr Burchell and the reform of Ephraim Jenkinson under the Vicar's influence. All of these elements come together in the final chapters of the book.

However, in spite of the skill with which these are all brought together at the end, the development of the story depends to a great degree upon unlikely coincidence, contrived situations and the intervention of fate. A list of some of these occurrences will make the point clear:

(1) The Vicar's loss of his income in Chapter 2 is obviously a means of removing him from Wakefield to the Thornhill estate.

(2) Sir William Thornhill's sustained disguise as Mr Burchell is unbelievable.

(3) The speed with which the Vicar suffers his misfortunes and the timing of the disasters are contrived as in the episode in Chapter 22 when he arrives home from a long journey just in time to see his house go up in flames.

(4) Sir William Thornhill's arrival in time to save Sophia from the clutches of his nephew, as reported in Chapter 30, is improbable.

(5) The fortunate encounter between the Vicar and Ephraim Jenkinson seems too good to be true.

(6) The arrival of all the leading characters in the prison in the final chapters and the rapid rise of the Vicar's fortunes is totally beyond belief.

But to judge a work like *The Vicar of Wakefield* strictly according to realistic standards would be to misunderstand its author's intentions. Obviously Goldsmith himself was aware of these apparent defects as his advertisement to the work seems to prove. On one level *The Vicar of Wakefield* has elements of the fairy tale about it. In this kind of fable we know that everything will come right in the end and we do not expect that the world of the writer's imagination should operate according to the laws of the real world. On another level the book often seems to be a parody of certain kinds of romantic fiction. By employing such formulas as unlikely disguise, wonderful coincidences and the happy intervention of fate, Goldsmith made fun of the elements which were commonplace in much contemporary writing. Indeed *The Vicar of Wakefield* is a more puzzling, complex and interesting work than any straightforward summary of its plot could ever suggest.

What insights into English life do we get from *The Vicar of Wakefield?*

A novel is not an historical document in the strict sense of the term. It is a work of the imagination and, as such, transmutes the real world in complex ways. Nevertheless, in a work like *The Vicar of Wakefield* the author to some extent used the social and historical realities as a basis for his imaginary world. But we should always be wary of a too easy and specific identification of the real and the imaginary.

In *The Vicar of Wakefield*, as in his famous poem *The Deserted Village* (1770), Goldsmith creates a picture of an idyllic rural community. This idyllic world of the first half of the novel has played a large part in the book's popularity with generations of readers. It is a quiet peaceful world where men live in accordance with the rhythms of nature. Old customs and traditions are preserved (see Chapters 4 and 11). The Vicar occupies a place of importance in the community next to the local Squire who owns the land on which the farmers live and work. The extent of such people's world is very small by twentieth-century standards. The journey which the Vicar and his family make from Wakefield to the Thornhill estate in Chapter 3 takes two days. Yet the distance is only seventy miles and the Vicar tells us that the family 'had hitherto never been above ten [miles] from home'. Because of the slowness and difficulty of travel the wayside inn was a very useful and necessary establishment as we realise from reading many episodes in the novel.

Squire Thornhill's despotic treatment of the Vicar may not have been typical of the way most rural landlords behaved. But it probably gives an accurate picture of the way such a powerful man could misuse his powers if it suited him to do so.

The account of prison life and the Vicar's criticism of the penal system in Chapters 25–32 reflect Goldsmith's own knowledge of and dissatisfaction with this system. Goldsmith is probably speaking directly through the mouth of the Vicar in Chapter 27 when he makes these dissatisfactions specific.

One other episode in the book is of particular interest. In Chapter 20 George Primrose gives a short but graphic account of the period which he spent in London trying to make his living as a writer. This is also based upon Goldsmith's own early experience in London and it offers a vivid glimpse of the hardships which many young writers must have suffered as apprentices in 'Grub Street'.

Consider the use of disguises in *The Vicar of Wakefield*

The Vicar of Wakefield abounds in disguises. Many of the characters go to great lengths to conceal their true identity. In Chapter 3 we first encounter the eccentric Sir William Thornhill disguised as Mr Burchell. He incredibly manages to hide his real identity until the final chapters of the novel. Ephraim Jenkinson adopts a series of disguises in order to cheat people of their money before he reveals his true identity in the prison episode. Several minor characters adopt false identities. For example, there are the fashionable ladies who offer to employ Olivia and Sophia in order to lure them into the grasp of Squire Thornhill. There is also the butler who assumes the role of his master and engages Dr Primrose in a political debate. Even the ballad which Sir William Thornhill recites is about a young man who pretends to be a hermit and regains his beloved in that assumed role.

Looked at realistically most of these disguises seem highly unlikely. This is particularly the case with regard to Sir William's role as Mr Burchell. It appears incredible that he is able to go about his own estates for so long without someone recognising him. However, it is clear that such a judgement is inappropriate to the logic of Goldsmith's fiction. Viewed within the perspective of the work as a whole we can see that these physical disguises point to the central theme of the book. This is the theme of the divergence between appearances and reality.

In the novel Goldsmith shows that a person's exterior appearance often conceals the hidden reality of his moral nature. He also highlights the ease with which even sensible people are fooled into mistaking a false show of manners and civility for good breeding. This is particularly apparent in those episodes in which the Primroses reject Mr Burchell (Sir William Thornhill) and court the favour of his nephew, the evil Squire Thornhill. On the other hand, Ephraim Jenkinson's true nature is constantly belied by his life-style as a confidence trickster. It is significant, moreover, that Dr Primrose is so often mistaken in his judgement of human motives and behaviour.

In his concern with the folly of making hard and fast moral judgements based only upon the superficial aspects of a person's behaviour Goldsmith was dealing with one of the great themes in literature. This theme is central to many of the greatest works of the imagination from Chaucer and Shakespeare to Jane Austen and Charles Dickens.

Discuss the portrayal of Dr Primrose's family

Dr Primrose is the most important and interesting character in Goldsmith's story. He is the only one who has something of the complexity of a real human being. His wife and children, on the other hand, are stylised or 'flat' characters. They think and act in limited and predictable ways throughout the story. They are much the same at the end as they were at the beginning. They never change or develop with experience.

Dr Primrose's eldest son, George, has many of his father's best qualities. He is honest and courageous and has a strong sense of honour. His career in London was clearly modelled on that of Goldsmith himself as a young man. However, he is less important as a character than as a device in the complicated workings of the plot. Moses, the Vicar's fourth child, is likewise a very 'flat' creation. He is a curious mixture of youth and maturity, wisdom and innocence. He supports the family when his father is imprisoned and shows moral and physical courage.

Both Dr Primrose's daughters, Olivia and Sophia, are necessary in the novel's plot. Yet, as characters, they are very stylised. Olivia, the more beautiful of the two, is vain and silly. Her seduction by Squire Thornhill is central to the whole story. Sophia, by contrast, is modest and unworldly. She is rewarded for her virtue by marriage to Sir William Thornhill. The two Primrose girls, however, are typical of 'stock' female characters found in much of the romantic fiction written in the eighteenth century.

The Vicar's wife, Deborah Primrose, is described by her husband in the opening chapter as 'a good natured notable woman' of limited but adequate education. However, Dr Primrose often unwittingly reveals many of the more serious shortcomings in his wife's character. She is over-ambitious for her daughters and is willing to sacrifice anything that happens to get in the way of their marriage prospects. She cares little for Squire Thornhill's bad reputation and unfairly insults Mr Burchell. She is often sharp-tongued and bad tempered. Sometimes she appears foolish and shallow as in the episode in which she insists upon riding the horse to church and in her attempts to make Squire Thornhill confess his interest in Olivia. In general, she lacks her husband's spontaneous generosity and charity as we see in her reception of Olivia after her return from Squire Thornhill.

It should be stressed, however, that Goldsmith's portrayal of such 'stock' characters does not reflect any shortcoming in his art. He was, to a great extent, parodying the very fictional form which he employed in writing his story and his stylised characterisation was integral to his larger ironic intentions in the novel.

Part 5

Suggestions for further reading

The text

For anyone who would like to read some of Goldsmith's other works there is a generous selection from his poetry, prose works, and plays in:
Goldsmith Selected Works, edited by Richard Garnett, Nonesuch Press, London, 1969.
The best modern edition of Goldsmith is *The Complete Works of Oliver Goldsmith* edited by Arthur Friedman, Oxford University Press, Oxford, 5 vols, 1966.

Criticism

JEFFARES, A.N.: *Oliver Goldsmith*, Writers and their Work, No. 107, Longmans, London, 1959, is a good short study of Goldsmith's life and writings.
GINGER, JOHN: *The Notable Man: The Life and Times of Oliver Goldsmith*, London, 1977, gives a detailed account of Goldsmith's life and the period in which he lived.

The author of these notes

BRIAN DONNELLY was educated at the University of Essex and St Mary's College of Education, Twickenham. He was a lecturer in English literature at the University of Aarhus, Denmark, from 1972 to 1976, and is presently lecturing in English at Carysfort College, Dublin. His publications include a short history of Ireland, a critical anthology of Irish drama and several articles in the field of Anglo-Irish literature. He has also worked on the production of programmes about Ireland for Danish radio and television. At the moment he is engaged in research for a short work on the literature about the British Raj in India.

The first 100 titles

CHINUA ACHEBE	*Arrow of God* *Things Fall Apart*
JANE AUSTEN	*Northanger Abbey* *Pride and Prejudice* *Sense and Sensibility*
ROBERT BOLT	*A Man For All Seasons*
CHARLOTTE BRONTË	*Jane Eyre*
EMILY BRONTË	*Wuthering Heights*
ALBERT CAMUS	*L'Etranger (The Outsider)*
GEOFFREY CHAUCER	*Prologue to the Canterbury Tales* *The Franklin's Tale* *The Knight's Tale* *The Nun's Priest's Tale* *The Pardoner's Tale*
SIR ARTHUR CONAN DOYLE	*The Hound of the Baskervilles*
JOSEPH CONRAD	*Nostromo*
DANIEL DEFOE	*Robinson Crusoe*
CHARLES DICKENS	*David Copperfield* *Great Expectations*
GEORGE ELIOT	*Adam Bede* *Silas Marner* *The Mill on the Floss*
T.S. ELIOT	*The Waste Land*
WILLIAM FAULKNER	*As I Lay Dying*
F. SCOTT FITZGERALD	*The Great Gatsby*
E.M. FORSTER	*A Passage to India*
ATHOL FUGARD	*Selected Plays*
MRS GASKELL	*North and South*

WILLIAM GOLDING	*Lord of the Flies*
OLIVER GOLDSMITH	*The Vicar of Wakefield*
THOMAS HARDY	*Jude the Obscure* *Tess of the D'Urbervilles* *The Mayor of Casterbridge* *The Return of the Native* *The Trumpet Major*
L.P. HARTLEY	*The Go-Between*
ERNEST HEMINGWAY	*For Whom the Bell Tolls* *The Old Man and the Sea*
ANTHONY HOPE	*The Prisoner of Zenda*
RICHARD HUGHES	*A High Wind in Jamaica*
THOMAS HUGHES	*Tom Brown's Schooldays*
HENRIK IBSEN	*A Doll's House*
HENRY JAMES	*The Turn of the Screw*
BEN JONSON	*The Alchemist* *Volpone*
D.H. LAWRENCE	*Sons and Lovers* *The Rainbow*
HARPER LEE	*To Kill a Mocking-Bird*
SOMERSET MAUGHAM	*Selected Short Stories*
HERMAN MELVILLE	*Billy Budd* *Moby Dick*
ARTHUR MILLER	*Death of a Salesman* *The Crucible*
JOHN MILTON	*Paradise Lost I & II*
SEAN O'CASEY	*Juno and the Paycock*
GEORGE ORWELL	*Animal Farm* *Nineteen Eighty-four*
JOHN OSBORNE	*Look Back in Anger*
HAROLD PINTER	*The Birthday Party*
J.D. SALINGER	*The Catcher in the Rye*
SIR WALTER SCOTT	*Ivanhoe* *Quentin Durward*

WILLIAM SHAKESPEARE	*A Midsummer Night's Dream*
	Antony and Cleopatra
	Coriolanus
	Cymbeline
	Hamlet
	Henry IV Part I
	Henry V
	Julius Caesar
	King Lear
	Macbeth
	Measure for Measure
	Othello
	Richard II
	Romeo and Juliet
	The Merchant of Venice
	The Tempest
	The Winter's Tale
	Troilus and Cressida
	Twelfth Night
GEORGE BERNARD SHAW	*Androcles and the Lion*
	Arms and the Man
	Caesar and Cleopatra
	Pygmalion
RICHARD BRINSLEY SHERIDAN	*The School for Scandal*
JOHN STEINBECK	*Of Mice and Men*
	The Grapes of Wrath
	The Pearl
ROBERT LOUIS STEVENSON	*Kidnapped*
	Treasure Island
JONATHAN SWIFT	*Gulliver's Travels*
W.M. THACKERAY	*Vanity Fair*
MARK TWAIN	*Huckleberry Finn*
	Tom Sawyer
VOLTAIRE	*Candide*
H.G. WELLS	*The History of Mr Polly*
	The Invisible Man
	The War of the Worlds
OSCAR WILDE	*The Importance of Being Earnest*